FOOTBALL:

A Love Story

EMORY HUNT JR.
TURRON DAVENPORT - GENE CLEMONS
BRANDON HOWARD - CHRIS JAMES

FOREWORD BY: MATT WALDMAN

Cover Photo: Football Gameplan LLC
Cover Design and Typesetting: Football Gameplan Publishing/Football Gameplan LLC

Davenport, Turron
Clemons, Gene
Howard, Brandon
Hunt, Emory
James, Christopher

First Printing: 2015
Football: A Love Story
ISBN-10: 0990551229
ISBN-13: 978-0-9905512-2-5
Copyright © 2015 by Football Gameplan Publishing/Football Gameplan LLC

Football Gameplan Publishing/Football Gameplan LLC
Washington Township, NJ 07676
info@footballgameplan.com

www.footballgameplan.com

Ordering Information:
Special discounts are available on quantity purchases by corporations, associations, educators and others. For details, contact Emory Hunt at ehunt@footballgameplan.com

U.S. trade bookstores and wholesalers: Please contact Football Gameplan Publishing - info@footballgameplan.com

Photo Credits

page 2 - North Carolina A&T State University Athletics
page 7 - Lamar University Athletics
page 13 - Richard Svaleson/NDSU Athletics
page 16 - Louisiana College Athletics
page 22 - Arizona State University Athletics
page 29 - Marshall University Athletics
page 32 - Eric Paull/University of Idaho Athletics
page 34 - Bob Cornell/Colgate University Athletics
page 37 - Scott Donaldson/South Alabama Athletics Media Relations
page 39 - USAFA Athletics
page 41 - Majors Media & Management
page 46 - Montreal Alouettes Media Relations
page 49 - BuffaloBills.com
page 51 - AP Photo/Rick Havner
page 54 - Chris OMeara/AP
page 56 - Rich Lam/UBC Athletics
page 58 - John Blackie/University of West Florida Athletics
page 63 - Texas Southern University Athletics
page 65 - Cumberland University Athletics
page 70 - Washington University Athletics
page 73 - Carnegie Mellon University Athletics
page 76 - Garden City Community College Athletics
page 78 - Oklahoma Baptist University Athletics
page 80 - Stephanie Zollshan/Berkshire Eagle Staff
page 82 - Georgia Military College Athletics
page 84 - Arizona Rattlers
page 86 - Otto Greule Jr/Getty Images North America
page 88 - Kim Klement-USA TODAY Sports
page 90 - Jeff Harwell/University of Akron Athletics
page 93 - Lake Forest College Athletics
page 96 - Bowling Green State University Athletics
page 98 - Redlands Sports Information
page 102 - University of Chicago Athletics
page 105 - Tease Marketing
page 110 - Vinny Dusovic
page 116 - Cam Tucker/Metro News Canada
page 118 - Jim Thompson/Albuquerque Journal
page 121 - Dyann Busse/North Carolina Central University Athletics
page 123 - Razorbacks Communications
page 125 - Dennis Carter
page 128 - Bridgewater College Athletics
page 130 - Anthony Becht Football Camp
page 132 - Cindy Ord/Getty Images North America
page 134 - George Bridges/MCT
page 136 - Christian Petersen/Getty Images North America

Photo Credits (Continued)

page 138 - Peter Mills/CBC
page 143 - Fresno State University Athletics/Geoff Thurner, Copyright 2014.
page 147 - Gino Payne
page 149 - LSUsports.net, LSU Athletics Publications
page 151 - Southern University Athletics
page 153 - Montreal Alouettes/Rogerio Barbosa
page 155 - Louis Lopez
page 157 - Dave Argyle
page 163 - Jonathan Daniel/Getty Images
page 169 - Cal Sport Media/AP
page 171 - Washington University Athletics
page 176 - NFL Alumni
page 181 - Mike Coppola/Getty Images North America
page 183 - Colorado State University Athletic Communications
page 186 - Arizona Cardinals
page 188 - Ethan Miller/Getty Images
page 190 - Mark Plank/Carroll College Athletics
page 193 - MICHAEL CONROY / Associated Press
page 195 - University of North Alabama Athletics
page 198 - East Mississippi Community College Athletics
page 200 - Las Vegas Outlaws
page 206 - Mississippi College Athletics
page 218 - Arena Football League
page 223 - Tim Peterson/Mid Valley Times
page 225 - Scouting Academy.com
page 228 - Marisha Camp/Huffington Post
page 235 - University of West Georgia Athletics
page 237 - Minnesota Vikings
page 243 - Jared Dort/Yuma Sun

All other photos are property of the individual owners, submitted for use in the book.

Special thanks to those coaches, players, analysts and executives that are featured in this book.

The following interviews were conducted and transcribed by the members of the Football Gameplan staff

Contents

19. Tom Higgins - Head Coach, Montreal Alouettes *46*

20. Chris Palmer - Senior Offensive Assistant, Buffalo Bills *49*

21. Charlie Coiner - Founder, 1st Down Technologies LLC *51*

22. Mike Singletary - Pro Football Hall of Fame Linebacker *54*

23. Blake Nill - Head Coach, University of British Columbia *56*

24. Pete Shinnick - Head Coach, University of West Florida *58*

25. Denauld Brown - Head Coach, Munich (Germany) Cowboys *60*

26. Kevin Ramsey - Defensive Coordinator, Alabama State University *63*

27. Brad Bustle - Offensive Line Coach, Cumberland University *65*

28. Turron Davenport - Baltimore Times, Football Gameplan Analyst *68*

29. Larry Kindbom - Head Coach, Washington University-St. Louis *70*

30. Rich Lackner - Head Coach, Carnegie Mellon University *73*

31. Jeffrey Sims - Head Coach, Garden City C.C. *76*

32. Chris Jensen - Head Coach, Oklahoma Baptist University *78*

33. Aaron Kelton - Head Coach, Williams College *80*

34. Bert Williams - Head Coach, Georgia Military College *82*

35. Kevin Guy - Head Coach, Arizona Rattlers *84*

36. Ed Reed - Retired NFL Player *86*

37. Steve Smith Sr. - Baltimore Ravens, Wide Receiver *88*

38. Terry Bowden - Head Coach, University of Akron *90*

75. Donna Wilkinson - Running Back, D.C. Divas *178*

76. Chris Canty - Defensive Lineman, Baltimore Ravens *181*

77. Mike Bobo - Head Coach, Colorado State University *183*

78. Ralph Brown II - Retired NFL Defensive Back,College Fball Analyst *186*

79. Aaron Garcia - Head Coach, Las Vegas Outlaws *188*

80. Mike Van Diest - Head Coach, Carroll College *190*

81. Howard Mudd - Retired NFL Offensive Line Coach *193*

82. Bobby Wallace - Head Coach, University of North Alabama *195*

83. Marcus Wood - Offensive Coordinator, East Mississippi C.C. *198*

84. Mike Lewis - Defensive End, Las Vegas Outlaws *200*

85. Eric Bartel - Co-Owner/Partner, Financial Coaching LLC *203*

86. John Bland - Head Coach, Mississippi College *206*

87. Brennan Marion - Offensive Assistant, Arizona State University *209*

88. Jim Light - Special Assistant Coach, Dakota High School (MI) *214*

89. Alberta Fitcheard-Brydson - Wide Receiver, Dallas Elite *216*

90. Scott Butera - Commissioner, Arena Football League *218*

91. Alex Kirby - Football Coach & Author *220*

92. Bob McMillen - Head Coach, Los Angeles Kiss *223*

93. Ken Flajole - Former NFL Defensive Coordinator *225*

FOREWORD

I love football. As a latchkey kid growing up in Cleveland, Ohio and, later, Atlanta, Georgia, football was as regular a part of my day as brushing my teeth. All I needed was another willing person and a ball— and we weren't picky about the ball: A Wilson with tattered laces and its dimples scuffed bald; a Nerf that paid a hefty neighborhood tax to the dog down the street; or even a stray Buster Brown would do.

Don't laugh. It had laces, you could throw a spiral with it, and it didn't hurt too much if you landed on it.

The depths of my love for football began so early in life that I planned my truancy days around the game. I scheduled "pre-skip" visits to the elementary school library so I could spend my day off reading stories about the exploits of Red Grange, George Halas, Jim Brown, Sammy Baugh and Deacon Jones to the bewildered family parakeet.

Although I played the game religiously until adulthood, my football life wasn't a straight path. The sum of my experience with the organized version was begging my way onto a Pop Warner team a month into the season after my family moved to Atlanta. Football was my dream, music lessons, competitions, and eventually, scholarship offers were my reality. But true love never dies. Decades later, and my musical aspirations miles away in the rear view mirror, I was climbing the corporate ladder when football came calling. A pre-draft analysis on Villanova runner Brian Westbrook inspired me to use my training to produce a scouting process rooted in best practices for film evaluation.

The Rookie Scouting Portfolio is now 11 seasons old and it has become a conversation starter for meaningful engagement about the game with former pros, college coaches, major media, NFL scouts, and NFL management. The RSP publication, blog, and YouTube channel has opened doors to contribute at *Footballguys, Football Outsiders, The New York Times,* and podcast appearances with *ESPN* and Ross Tucker. It's not the path I would have ever imagined for my life, especially as that kid skipping school to share the exploits of Johnny Blood to his pet bird.

This is the arc of my football love story. It's an honor to share it with you as an introduction to Football: A Love Story, Emory Hunt's heartfelt chronicle of the game through the eyes of the people who have committed their lives to it. As unusual as my love affair with the game seems, Hunt's book reveals that any lasting relationship with football is a story that is both unique and universal.

Hunt and Football Gameplan contributors Gene Clemons, Turron Davenport, Brandon Howard and Christopher James capture these qualities about the game and the people in love with it—many of them whose contributions have inspired millions to begin love affairs of their own. The stories in this book are a testament to football's standing as America's passion.

When approached as intended, football is a game brimming with intelligence, creativity, discipline, emotion, and humility. It challenges its students to develop these qualities in themselves in order to meet the game's highest standards. Football humbles me with each passing year, because the more I learn the less I feel I know.

Hunt and his team educate and entertain with a dedication to football's highest principles in all of their work. When it comes to staying true to his process, there are few football analysts who possess Hunt's integrity. It didn't take long for me to become a fan.

After you read Football: A Love Story, so will you.

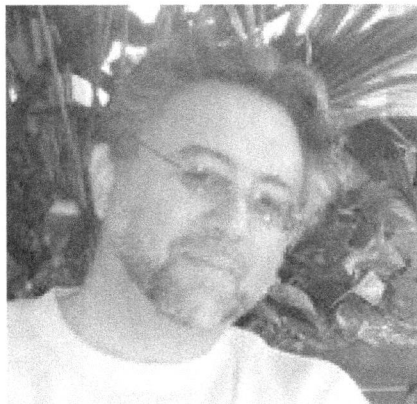

Matt Waldman
Magazine Journalist
Rookie Scouting Portfolio Author
@MattWaldman
www.mattwaldmanrsp.com

They say that love is everlasting and passion is only in spurts, but to those involved with the game of football, the two emotions are one in the same. So much so that it hurts. But we then forgive, forget, reconcile and heal before the next play starts so we can do it all over again.

Football is more than a game to us and we're here to tell you why.

Here are our stories.

"I told my momma in the sixth grade I wanted to be a football coach. By that right, I'm one of the lucky ones. Guys I grew up with wanted to be professional football players.
I wanted to coach. I had a couple of coaches I really liked, and I said I want to be able to do that. I'm living the dream."

- Rod Broadway
  Head Coach, North Carolina A&T
  @ncataggies

WILLIE ROBINSON
HEAD COACH: LUEBECK COUGARS
WWW.LUEBECK-COUGARS.DE - @LUEBECKCOUGARS

Growing up in my household, I was the only boy; I had 2 sisters. I didn't have a father figure in my life because my mom didn't marry my father. She married my sister's father, but he wasn't around either. I think as a child, I was always aggressive. So even as a kid, I always felt as though I was misunderstood because I didn't have many outlets. It was very hard on me when I was young because I was looking for a way to release that aggression, to spin all of this energy I had built up. At the time, I started watching football and growing up in D.C., I was a big fan of the Washington Redskins. I was the type of kid who tried to emulate everything I saw on TV. So, watching football, I remember I used to go and grab a duffle bag, fill it up with all of the dirty or clean clothes, and I would just stand it up in the corner and go tackle it. So, I was really drawn into the game from the standpoint that it was just exciting. It was something that allowed me to express myself. I would go outside, play with the kids in the street and I would love it because playing the game, I felt free. It was the only thing I wanted to do, even at a young age.

I played other sports in the neighborhood like basketball. But I was more interested in the physical part of it; so it didn't give me that same feeling that football did. At that point, my mom took me across the way to the CYO team and signed me up for football. And from that day on, I felt like it was God sent, like God sent football to her to 'give' to me and she never had to worry about her son again. Like I said before, I was the only boy, but at that point in time football put me around 100 boys. So I was around a lot of boys, a lot of coaches, which was vital because of the encouragement and direction they gave me. It made feel special. I became addicted to the game.

Growing up in a single-parent home, the struggle was real. Everybody in my family, dealt with some sort of drug addiction. It was rough to see my mom in tough situations. In the community, football was my way to get away from what the other guys were doing in the neighborhood. Guys were either chasing girls or dabbling in minor drug dealing. But what I found interesting was that the guys in the neighborhood that were doing all of those things, seemed to treat the guys that played sports a different kind of way. It wasn't peer pressure to come out and join them in what they were doing; it was like "Yo...that's the boy that plays football." So I took honor in that because it sort of gave me a safety net and also protected me because the guys in the neighborhood saw that in me. I didn't have to worry about anything happening to me that would just happen to a stray kid.

I can think back to two big things that happened to me, which really sticks with me even today. The first organized game I got to play in, they gave out our equipment the day before the game, and I remember walking home from practice in full gear. I wanted everybody to see me because I felt like the man. That night, something happened to me and this was the point where I felt like God put something in my life that would take me to where I am today. My cousins, who were older than me, were bad influences to be honest. Since it was the night before the game, I couldn't sleep so I decided to go and hang out with them. And these guys are just terrorizing things; doing stuff like throwing rocks, trying to turn over cars, dumb things like that. So, eventually the police are coming around and my cousin says 'here comes the police.' So as I turn around to run, I run smack into a pole. I still have the gash on my forehead today to prove it. I'm bleeding profusely. I finally was able to make onto the rooftop of one of the buildings and I have the big knot on my forehead that's bleeding; I have my first game the next day and I all I could do was just wonder to myself, what the hell am I doing? Praying to God to please let me make it home and play in my game tomorrow. The fact that I still have the scar to this day is my daily reminder to stay on task and do the right thing.

Football always had my back. I went to 10 different elementary schools as a kid. We moved around a lot. From going from homeless shelter, to homeless shelter, to going live with family members, we were constantly on the move. No matter what we had going on, I felt that football was always my way out and it saved me. I always feel that with all of that negativity that was happening around me, if football wasn't there to occupy my time and mind, I could've easily ended up in jail or dead. That's why I hold this game so close to my heart.

I think what made me stay connected to the game, was going back to what first drew me into the game. Football was God's gift to me. It allowed me to accomplish many things. I'm the first in my family to go and graduate from college. Football was given to me as a vehicle. My adopted dad told me that football is not a means to an end but a mean to attain a means. To me, football was something God gave me when he didn't give me anything else. So for me, a lot of people talk about their love and passion for the game, but my love for the game, from playing to now coaching and giving back, is coming from somewhere deep down in my heart. Because it wasn't a motivation out of money or out of fame, it was used as a tool to survive. There's nothing I feel would ever draw me away from the game. Although I have a college education; although I speak 3 different languages, the only thing that God gave me that was pure, to me at least, was the game of football.

I'm not in this game to make money; I'm in this game because it's who I am; it's who I wake up to be. I don't ever envision myself getting a 'regular job' or anything like that; I think about how can I become a better coach? How can I impact the game that has given me so much? Coaching is something that I feel that I'm compelled to do. The way the game has changed though, you don't really get to talk to people about what the game means to you because the intentions and what the game is about has changed. There are still some people, like myself, that the game is pure to. If I could die in any way, I'd rather die like this, doing what I'm doing.

CAREY BAILEY

DEFENSIVE LINE COACH: LAMAR UNIVERSITY

WWW.LAMARCARDINALS.COM - @CAREYBAILEY

When I was in the 4th grade, one of my good friend's dad was the coach of the little league team in my area, so I went out for the team. I was 10 years old, playing with the 10-12 year olds and I was just dominating. The problem was that there was a weight limit and I was over that limit for that age group, so I couldn't play. I was 120lbs, so for 2 years I just practiced with the team. When my grandmother died, she left my mom a nice chunk of change so we were able to move to another area, out of the trailer park and into a nice house, new area and a new school district. And the coach at the time at the new junior high school, he and my dad worked together. So I was able to finally play and again was dominating the competition. As a young kid, having success with the game, made me fall in love with it. I was having success because I was an angry kid, my mom and dad divorced when I was 5 years old, so football gave me that outlet to release all of that anger and frustration.

What's funny is that I didn't look for football as a career, it sort of came looking for me. When I was in college at the University of Tennessee, my major was Criminal Justice and I wanted to be a federal marshal. Let me give you a little bit of background. The 1986-87 recruiting class, I was one of the top 4 lineman in the state of West Virginia. I had been to every camp at West Virginia University. I knew everything about the Mountaineers and their program, every coach, basically everything. Bill Kirelawich, who's now the defensive line coach at the University of Arizona, he was the defensive line coach at the time and his wife was my 8th grade math teacher. I mean... so I was well connected with the university. My dad played basketball at West Virginia. My mother went to West Virginia and she was the first black president of the general alumni association and was on the athletic council. So, I was entrenched with my bloodlines so-to-speak in West Virginia. But, I decided not to go to WVU, but instead to Tennessee because I felt that people here (West Virginia) know me, so I need to go somewhere else and make a name and prove myself because I'm a challenge type of guy.

So going into my senior year at Tennessee, I got a call from Don Nehlen the head coach at the time at West Virginia. Coach Nehlen said that he may have a graduate assistant spot open this time next year and he would like to bring me back, would I be interested? I said, sure! The reason why I said sure was because at the time, my father worked in corrections and when I told him that I wanted to be a federal marshal, he was like now isn't a good time to do so.

So I'm like sure, I'll go and be a G.A. and work on my Master's. Now the 3 seasons prior to me getting there, WVU wasn't very good. I went in as the Strength and Conditioning coach working under Al Johnson who's a master strength and conditioning coach. Al comes back, and we go undefeated! We were 11-0 but lost to Florida in the Sugar Bowl. So the other G.A., Tim Newsome, his time was up and they brought in another guy in Kevin Ramsey. And Ramsey told the coach that the best G.A. candidate to replace Newsome was down in the weight room. Next thing you know, I get a call and I'm then working with the secondary. So I was actually just getting into the coaching part as a way to get my Master's and doing something else, but football pulled me back in. Once I started coaching, I realized that I was a good communicator, an effective teacher and the game slowed down for me from a coaching standpoint. Those were some of the things that I was able to see, which allowed me to be successful over the years. The longer I was in it, the more I fell in love with it. That's how my path got started with coaching; it wasn't a situation where I was like 'oh, I'll go be a player and then I'll get into coaching.' It was like fate brought me to it, in order to get me to where I am now.

When I was at Tennessee, and don't get me wrong, I love Coach Johnny Majors to this day and I've learned a lot from him in terms of how to go about your business and be a professional. But the one thing about Tennessee that I didn't like when I was a player was that there weren't many coaches that you could go to if you had an issue. They were all about ball. If you wanted to see Coach Majors, you had to schedule an appointment with him. You couldn't just walk into his office, unless there was an issue. Everything was football and it was your responsibility to take care of everything else. So, when I got into coaching, I always told myself that I wasn't going to be one of those guys that only talks to his players or the players around him, only about football, because life is so much more complex. Football only last for, if you break it down over the course of an 11 game season, 660 minutes. That being said, for me, understanding where I came from, where since I was 5 my father was absent because of the divorce, a lot of the players knew that I came a similar background as them. A lot of times, the first authoritative male figure for these guys will be a coach. So I wanted to make sure that whatever knowledge I had that allowed me to get through and navigate life without getting into trouble, I wanted to pass it on to the next generation so that they could be successful and not be a detriment to society.

There are a lot of guys that I played ball with both in high school and in college, that once they stopped playing ball, they lost their identity. They became so encapsulated to what they were on the field, that they lost sight of what they were individually. So, I try to talk to guys about keeping things in perspective because at the end of the day, the easier it is for me to navigate through life just makes it easier for me to be successful on the field or in any endeavor that I choose to partake in.

If my football epitaph could read anything, I'd want to say that Coach Bailey kept it real. If they put that on my football tombstone, that would encapsulate my life. I'm very proud of the fact that I've never compromised myself as a man, myself as a black man, or myself as a coach when something was not right. If it's right, it's right and if it's wrong it's wrong and I've acted consistently and properly upon both.

JAMES WILLIAMS
HEAD COACH: BARCELONA BUFALS
WWW.BARCELONABUFALS.COM - @JAMES77WILLIAMS

Initially I wasn't playing football. I was playing baseball and basketball. My freshman year in high school, an older member of the football team used to tell me everyday 'hey man, you got to play football.' I never really considered it. I think one of the main things when I finally decided to join, it was mid-season and they let me join the team maybe because of my size, it was the camaraderie of the players and the family sense of the team that drew me in. I noticed that closeness right away. The film sessions, the workouts, the practices, I felt a bond there and it was different than any other team I had been on. In my sophomore year in high school, I made a transition to a different high school. I met one of the older guys on the team and he said 'hey, I'm committed to the University of Tennessee, and if I can help you in any way, your adjustment to the team, let me know.' That was a big thing for me because I was like 'wow, the University of Tennessee.' I never looked that far ahead. My vision was so shortsighted that I just really focused on the current season. I then realized that there was potential here if I just worked and developed myself.

As a player, it's the camaraderie amongst the team and having a huge group to be around is one of the things I love about the game of football. As a coach, I think it's the opportunity to serve and help others and to be a part of something that's bigger than yourself that pull you in. Just to see guys transform, be inspired to get better everyday and for them to see the result of their work, is something you love from that perspective. That's really inspiring for me. I want to be the guy that helped spread football to other countries, and helped kids around the world. Hands down. Bringing the game to new places, while helping the game grow to a point where it is in the Olympics; being a part of that is what I would want my impact on the game to be.

CHRIS KLIEMAN

HEAD COACH: NORTH DAKOTA STATE UNIVERSIT

WWW.GOBISON.COM - @COACHKLI

My dad was a coach and I was constantly around the game as a young guy, and really developed a passion for the sport. I remember going to the practices. I remember being in the locker room listening to his pre-game speeches. I just really loved the environment. Football had me always watching things on TV, always had me reading more about the game. Heck, I remember reading Knute Rockne books in middle school. That's how passionate I was about the game, and I credit my dad for that.

I've always loved football. From growing up, to high school and throughout college, I've always had that love. As far as coaching is concerned, it crept up on me pretty fast. I remember I graduated in December following my senior year, and at the time I was playing at Northern Iowa. I was fortunate to play for a guy named Terry Allen, who is a great mentor of mine. Also at the time, the athletic director was a guy by the name of Bob Bowlsby, who is now the commissioner of the Big XII, and I approached both guys and said that I don't know what I want to do, but I like to stay in football. There wasn't a graduate assistant job available at the time, but Bowlsby said 'hey, we're going to keep you on scholarship so you can take some graduate classes to see if this is what you want to do.' So Terry let me work with the guys that spring, I really enjoyed it and it gave me the opportunity to see if this was the path I want to pursue and the rest is history; and I've had an unbelievable journey.

On the field, I love the competitiveness of the game. I always wanted to compete, I always wanted to get better and I was one of those guys that always watched a ton film. I did the best I could in the weight room. I wasn't blessed to have tons of ability, but I was always going to put myself in position to be successful by knowing what the opponent was doing; helping other guys be in the right spot and get in position. I was kind of the quarterback of our defense in college, making all of the checks and calls, and as a player, I really enjoyed those things. From a coaching perspective, I really like the teaching element of it. I love interacting with the guys. To me, there's nothing more satisfying than seeing a player just execute a fundamental technique to perfection that we've worked on over, and over again. For me, the neat thing is to see the look of success on the players' face when they do a technique properly and it worked. It gives them great confidence.

As a coach, I hope my lasting impact would be that I was known as a great teacher of the game, that I was able to motivate guys and that I was approachable from the player's point of view. I see myself, as a players-coach and I know some school of thought is that you don't want to get 'that close' to the guys, but this is a different era of football. My philosophy has been to get to know the guys; to be a mentor to those guys; to be a leader to those guys. You want to be that guy that the players are not afraid to come and knock on your door to talk to you about academics, life or whatever.

STANLEY SMITH

Linebackers Coach: University of Arkansas-Pine Bluff
WWW.UAPBLIONSROAR.COM - @UAPBLIONSROAR

I can think back to when I was 11 years old in the 5th grade watching all of my older cousins play ball and I was the 5th cousin, and I admired them and I wanted to play. All of my other cousins ahead of me signed D1 scholarships. So I was kind of a pup sitting there waiting for my turn and I couldn't wait to get off of the leach. Once I got my opportunity as a freshman, I became a starter and never looked back. Funny part is that I went out for basketball one day and realized instantly that it wasn't for me. We had a rule in high school that if you quit a sport, you couldn't play any sport for a complete year. Good thing I was an exception to that rule and my coach continued to let me play football. I've just been a part of the game ever since.

During my sophomore year in college, I realized that I couldn't see myself doing anything other than football for my career. I played a lot as a true freshman and as a sophomore, so I saw that there was an opportunity for me to be able to further my career if I kept on this current track. And I put all of my focus and energy into accomplishing that goal. I had some opportunities to play professional ball, I played some Arena Football before injuries curtailed my career. But it was just a blessing to be able to have that chance to play at a high level, to call yourself a professional and I met some really good guys, both players and coaches along the way.

I can't begin to explain enough how much the camaraderie means to me, with regards to the game of football. Just to be on the same page, fighting and working for the same goal with your teammates is invaluable. If I'm looking at you directly in your eyes, I don't have to say a word because we are all on the same wavelength and have the same thought process. I don't think you can get that anywhere else. That type of brotherhood is irreplaceable. At the end of the day, when someone says the word football, or ask 'what does football mean to you?' the first and only thing that comes to mind is 'Team'. And for me, it doesn't get any simpler and more profound than that. We can do many things in life, but I felt as though football was my calling and I'm proud to say that I'm living the dream of exactly what I set out to do as a kid.

DAN HATMAN

DIRECTOR OF SCOUTING DEVELOPMENT

WWW.SCOUTINGACADEMY.COM - @DAN_HATMAN

I was very fortunate that time and circumstance gave me an opportunity. I broke into the NFL at 19 years old as a summer intern with the New York Giants. Truly a right place, right time type deal. They were having training camp at the University of Albany, which was where I went for undergrad; I had transitioned from walk-on to volunteer assistant coach and I was trying to work myself up that way. There was just something about a group of guys getting together and striving to accomplish things. Two things captivated me about this concept. The first was that it was the element of building up a group, the training and development of these young men in hopes of creating something greater than the individual. And second, the combative, competitive aspect of matching up a group of people going through the same exercise, and seeing who's better. Both of those things grabbed me really early in the process. Going from a relatively small program, like the University of Albany, to all of a sudden being an intern with the Giants. It was interesting going from the coaching and personnel side, to seeing a totally different way of how this can be done. One thing kind of rolled into another, going from a summer intern to a full-time intern; my first full year in the league, we're in the Super Bowl beating the New England Patriots and I got a Super Bowl ring. Needless to say, the bug sort of bit me right then. You get a ring, something that a lot of guys spend their whole career trying to get, and you get it in year one? My mindset switched to trying replicate that feeling, especially in a position where I can have an impact or have some sort of influence.

I think not having the opportunity to play collegiately for very long due to injury, that sort of thing left a bad taste in my mouth of something that wasn't fulfilled. That was a motivating factor to where now I get to pursue this and to continue to move forward in. I'm kind of a legacy-based guy in the sense, sort of like Bill Walsh and not like a football genius or anything like that but, in the sense that he has many branches to 'his' tree. When people talk about Bill Walsh, they always talk about his coaching tree. Well, that's what I kind of want. Right now I have 6 individuals that I've trained how to scout and they're now doing that for professional teams. Their work far supersedes what I have done for them, but just to know that I had an impact in helping them accomplish their dream, is something that I really enjoy. So I would like to look back and hoped that I've touched more lives in that manner.

BAKIAL JAMES "BJ" HALL

QUARTERBACK COACH, LARGO HIGH SCHOOL (FL)
FOUNDER & COACH - TEAM FLORIDA 7-ON-7
WWW.TEAMFLORIDAFOOTBALL.COM - @BJHALL5

Man I fell in love with football at 8 years old. My parents were both on drugs, so in my home, it was tough. I didn't like to be home, so I was always outside in the neighborhood. The only thing that made me happy was playing football and hanging out with friends. You can ask the guys I grew up with and they'll tell you that I was that kid skipping around the neighborhood at 8 o'clock on a Saturday morning with a football in my hand. Guys were like 'man lets play some video games' and I'm like nah, lets play football. That's the impact the game had on me and a lot of guys remember me as the kid that always carried a football around. That's when I fell in love with the game. I knew that if I was outside doing something that I loved, it made the things that were going on at home seem that much better.

I realized in college that football is what I wanted to be for my career. In high school, for me, it was similar to playing little league. It was fun. I didn't really understand how to take it seriously because I really wasn't coached that way. But when I got to college, it became tougher; I had to study more. So, at that level, you either you want to play it or you don't depending on the ingredients you get from the coaches. It's a lot of studying; a lot of waking up early for 5am workouts, so if you're not mentally tough in that aspect, you'd tend to say 'nah, this isn't what I want to do long term.' I didn't have a problem with that grind, so I wanted to take it to the next level of what this could be. Again, it was just another confirmation of my love of football.

If you take a look at my background, nothing was given to me. And I would hope people are able to say that I had tremendous work ethic, he loved the game and earned everything he got from it. I mean, most people would sit down and say that they're done with the game after some early setbacks, but I went through many trials and tribulations. Now I understand why I had to go through those things; it was to be able to tell a story and give back to the next generation coming up now and in the future.

TODD GRAHAM
HEAD COACH - ARIZONA STATE UNIVERSITY
WWW.THESUNDEVILS.COM - @COACHGRAHAMASU

I grew up in Texas. From the time that I could walk, football was a part of our culture. The game, I was taught, it was ingrained in me that it is the greatest game on earth because it emulated life. You have to be tough, disciplined and have great work ethic. It's a team sport. Not one guy, 11 guys have to play together for good things to happen. From the time that I can remember, I wanted to be a football player. The identity of every town, especially where I grew up, was in the football team. Character, smart, discipline and tough, the game teaches you so much about that. The game isn't easy. It's very physical and demanding. The training, there isn't a tougher sport that you can play. I was out in the pasture playing football with my brothers as long as I can remember.

I was an All American safety in college. I got to play at every level. It was a very brief time for me in the NFL, but that was the dream. I would still play today. They cut me so I had to go coach. Where I grew up, it was every boy's dream to be an NFL player and playing pro football. As a youngster as a tailback scoring touchdowns, the game became so much of who you are.

I knew when I went into college, my junior year, my family had never gone to college. Football was a game changer for me. I would not have been able to go to school if it wasn't for football. So many kids that I grew up with, if you didn't have something like that, you weren't able to go to college. I knew that I wanted to be a college football player, play in the NFL for as long as I can remember. I wanted to be a football coach because I wanted to spend my life around this game that I love so much. I like the grind, I like how tough it is and to me it emulates life. Sometimes my wife gets mad at me, she says that she's supposed to be the love of my life but she suspects that it's football. I will plead the fifth on that one.

What I love most about the game is Game Day. I can remember the locker room, the pageantry, the buildup, the electricity. High school football in Texas is pretty phenomenal. Stepping across the white lines, to be in the arena, the physicality of it, there's nothing like imposing your will on someone and physically dominating them. I loved the physicality of the game. I always played on great defenses that really put the pads on them. We did it within the framework of the rules.

I love how demanding it is. Not just the physical part of it, the mental aspect also. I still run out of the tunnel with our team and I still love it, the locker room, the buildup, the half time adjustments, and the fourth quarter stretch. We hit a hail mary, they called it the "Jail Mary" vs USC last year and the emotions and looks on our player's faces, there's nothing like it. I remember as a player, the last game that I played. It was hard, it was difficult because I love coaching and being around the game. It's awesome and I am blessed to get to do this but man, I miss the arena, I miss being a warrior. Football is a game where you have to have pretty strong intestinal fortitude. You're going to get knocked down. You're not going to win every battle. You learn to get back up and prepare and discipline. That's the key to being successful.

You learn how to handle adversity. That's one of the things that I still remember. I am 50 years old and I tell these kids that I still remember playing in a game and someone running a quick slant route. I remember the jersey number. It was #83 and I remember dropping that shoulder it was a bang bang play. I remember that. Just to get to feel what it feels like to do that again is something that I'd love to do. I am an intense competitor. I love that. I love it about the game, gameday, the run through, the sideline, there's just nothing like that when you make a play like that. The work, Vince Lombardi talks about the work, how you pour your heart and soul into it. Blood, sweat, you're battered and beaten but you are able to feel victorious. There's nothing like the competition on the gridiron. There is no other sport like it. I've obviously had a love affair with football for most of my life because it was ingrained in me. It has never let me down. It has always been good to me.

I would want my football epitaph to read, "He was a person who respected this game." I want to be known as someone who did it with heart and integrity, sportsmanship, also a fierce competitor. The press guide when I played for the St. Louis Cardinals had my name as a ferocious hitter. I would want to be known as a fierce competitor. I did things in honor, with integrity and sportsmanship. That was because I respected the game. Guys like Tom Landry, Roger Staubach, Joe Gibbs, just the respect. You could tell that I grew up a Cowboys fan; I hated Gibbs because he coached the Redskins but he had class and character. You can't just take from this game. It is a great game that should be respected with honor. You do that by playing the game the way it's supposed to be played, that's hard, tough and physical.

WILLIAM JORDEN, ESQ.
GENERAL COUNSEL - FOOTBALL GAMEPLAN

My dad initially drew me into the game of football. When I moved from California to New Orleans, I never played football. I didn't really care for it. I remember watching the Buffalo Bills play the New York Giants in the Super Bowl and that was my first experience of actually watching a football game. But when I came to Louisiana, my dad bought me a football and we threw it around in the yard. There was just something about that, which I really enjoyed. After awhile, I remember telling my dad that I wanted to go play little league football.

I always liked playing football, but it was probably when I was 15 years old that I really fell in love with the game. We were going up against one of the powerhouse programs in John Curtis, and for whatever reason I felt like I could compete verses the best of the best. I was consistently making plays at outside linebacker and I didn't feel like the game was moving too fast for me. So it was at that point, as well as the rest of that season, where I felt as though I grew into my own and felt that I could compete at a high level. And at that point, it was something I really wanted to do because I was good at it. What really kept me 'in' the game was seeing the type of man that football helped me become. While I think that all team sports help build character, the thing about football, especially at the college level, when you have those 5am workouts in the freezing cold, you're bear crawling, it helps test your mettle. It helps reveal your true character. It's funny because you do see people quit. I would always say that it wouldn't be me. Because I'll never start something, go this far, take this much of a beating to then go and turn my back on it. Wasn't happening. I know some guys will say that it was the winning that kept them in the game, but for me, I actually enjoyed the pain because it really did test you as a man.

If I had to write my own football epitaph, I'd want it to say that William Jorden played the game the right way, played it hard and didn't back down from a challenge; he may not have been the most athletic; he may not have been the fastest, or even the smartest but he had the work ethic and stick-to-itiveness to make a way. And through all of that, he was a real man in the game. Ultimately, that's what I'd want my lasting football legacy to be.

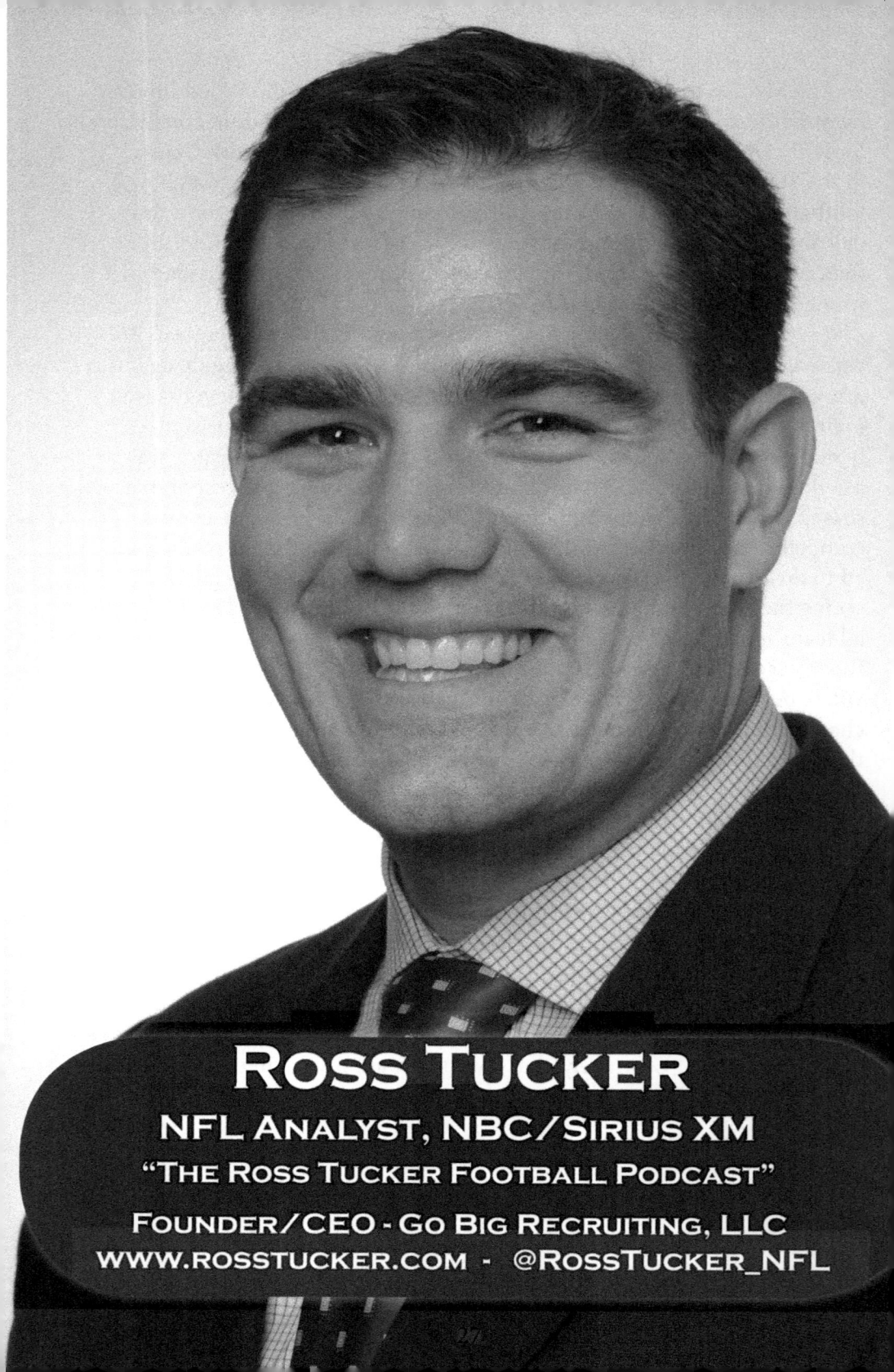

ROSS TUCKER

NFL Analyst, NBC/Sirius XM

"The Ross Tucker Football Podcast"

Founder/CEO - Go Big Recruiting, LLC
www.rosstucker.com - @RossTucker_NFL

My first memory in my entire life, I think I was 4 or 5 years old, my parents took me to a Penn State game and I just remember how big the stadium was. Walking in the actual stadium, seeing how green the grass was, seeing the colors of the Penn State uniform, I can remember saying to myself that this was awesome and I want to do this. I was hooked right then man. I remember in the '85 Orange Bowl, watching the whole thing and crying my eyes out when Penn State lost to Oklahoma. I was exposed to the game at a young age and I loved it immediately.

I didn't really know how far I could take it, with the game of football. I had an older sister who was 4 years older than me that was a cheerleader, so I was around the varsity football players a lot when I was in middle school. Which I believe are very formidable years. So, I hear these guys constantly talk about football long term, and I idolized these guys. I just decided then, that I would live my life with no regrets as far as football is concerned. I knew right then that football was my most favorite thing in the world to do. I said to myself that when I was a senior in high school, I wouldn't be the one to say 'I wish I'd done this or I'd wish I'd done that.' I'm going to be able to say; that I became the very best I could be at my most favorite thing in the world to do. So, I never really looked at it something that could be a long-term thing. I mean, I'd thought I'd go to Syracuse and work for ESPN, Sports Illustrated or something like that. I never thought about playing in college until I had a really good junior year and started getting recruiting letters. I had got a lot bigger that year as well, but still hadn't thought of it as a possibility. I knew I wanted to do something where sports, and more in particular, football was a big part of it.

Sometimes people cringe when I say this, but I just really embraced the physicality. And I miss the violence of the game. I miss trying to hit another human being as hard as I can. I miss that sensation. I miss knocking people over. Sometimes, I think people are afraid to admit or say that. I think that's a very primal instinct that a lot of us have and I think it's okay to embrace that. I really miss that about the game. Obviously, that takes a toll on your body and I'm glad for that reason I don't do it anymore. I'd pay a lot of money for 5 more snaps of high school football. If you were to tell me that I could go out there at night and play 5 more plays of a high school football game, wow... I'd pay a lot just for that sensation again. The good news is that, I kind of realized that when I was playing. I sort of knew how special it was and I never took it for granted. I hope people say that I loved the game as much as anyone ever has, and became the best player he possibly could be. I gave the game of football everything that I had and I got a whole lot back in return!

DOC HOLLIDAY

HEAD COACH - MARSHALL UNIVERSITY

WWW.HERDZONE.COM - @DOCMUFB

I've just always loved the game of football you know. I loved everything about it. I loved the competing, loved the winning part of it and everything that goes into it. As a player, I just felt like I wanted to coach and had an opportunity to get started at an early age, I got lucky and here I am today.

I don't think there's another game out there like the game of football. It's tough. There's nowhere to hide in this game and it's something that not everybody can do; and if you don't love this game and really love it in your heart, then football's tough because all the work that goes into just the opportunity to play. In our case, this year was fourteen games so you prepare 365 days a year for those fourteen opportunities and it's not easy. It's tough, it's physical, and you're gonna ache and you're gonna hurt and that's just the way the game is. And if you don't love it and have a big 'ole heart for it, then you will have a hard time surviving.

I have just a love of the game. I think that's critical. That is the hardest thing when recruiting kids today. I tell the story all the time when I went to the University of Florida. You put that big gator on your shirt and you think you've arrived and you think recruiting is going to really be easy, but in my mind at that point it became tougher. You had the opportunity to have access to all these so called five-star athletes that were all great players but, you had to find out was football really important to them, do they love the game. Was winning championships more important than not making the right decisions off the field, doing right and all those things? Because, I believe that's what separates the good teams from the teams that win championships. It's getting the type of players that are not only great players, but love all the work and everything that goes into it. I just think that's the biggest issue with the game today is that the ones that don't finish, think there's more things out there important to them than winning championships, and getting their college degree. Those kids are going to be the ones that don't make it. It's giving kids the opportunity to really grow up, become men and make something of themselves and football provided them with that opportunity. It bothers me all the time when all you hear is what's wrong with college football, well there's a hell of a lot of things right with it. There are a lot of examples of these types of kids out there because of college football. I've got example after example of kids out of Miami and the inner cities that without football, had no chance.

But because of football, it gives them the opportunity to get a college degree and make something of themselves and hopefully, at some point, maybe they go on and play in the NFL. But if they don't, they've gotten their degree and that's going to help them be successful for the rest of their life. Just for the last 35 plus years I've only recruited South Florida. Now since I've become the head coach, of course I recruit everywhere, but it's just example after example of kids that have had the opportunity because of football to be successful in life and to make something of themselves and that gives me more joy than anything else.

PAUL PETRINO
HEAD COACH - UNIVERSITY OF IDAHO
WWW.GOVANDALS.COM - @VANDALFOOTBALL

32

My dad was a coach, I was around it for a very long time and I knew from an early age that I wanted to play for a long time and then go right into coaching. I just knew it from the very start, again, just being around it all the time; all of his (Dad) practices and around the building a lot as a kid. I really loved playing the game, so when I was done playing, I knew I still wanted to be around it and that led me into coaching.

I love the competition of it all. Football is a physical, 'get-after-it' sport. It's more of a team sport than any other sport there is, to be honest. Everybody has to come together, everybody plays a role and it takes 11 guys to make a play work. Especially offensively, it takes those 11 guys to make it work every single time. I was an option quarterback, so I liked the physical combat, the competition and the hitting. Really, I love just everything about it.

As a coach, I would hope that all of the former players that I've worked with thought that I was a great teacher and a great motivator. Those are the two most important things that you have to get across. I hope they saw that I wanted to teach them life long lessons. And that is both on the field, getting them to be the best player that they can be; and also off the field, teaching them to become better dads, husbands, leaders or whatever they decide to go into. Whether it is owning their own company, being a doctor or lawyer, you just hope that the lessons they've learned in life, came from what you as a coach was able to give to them each and everyday.

DAN HUNT

HEAD COACH - COLGATE UNIVERSITY

WWW.GOCOLGATERAIDERS.COM - @COACHDANHUNT

I would say the initial draw to football for me, as it was probably for a lot of young kids, is just kind of what you did when you were young. Whether because it was the fall, you see the older kids playing for the Pop Warner in your town, or maybe it was because your older brother played, so initially, that's what drew me in. Once you start playing, I believe that of all of the youth sports, it's the one that best taught roles on a team. It's not like soccer, when you watch youth soccer, where it looks like a blob of 30 kids on a field trying to kick one ball. Baseball is very individual, you're up to bat by yourself, you're pitching by yourself, and the ball is hit to you by yourself, it's all solo. What I really liked about football was that, you really played WITH your friends and learned about being a teammate, and having a role.

I think I knew in high school that football was all I wanted to do. I really respected my high school football coach. I guess it was really naïve of me to think that's what they did all day was coaching football. I knew right then, that is what I wanted to do. I always enjoyed the strategy and teaching of it, even as a player in high school. I believe one of the common traits of a lot of coaches, especially a lot of the good coaches that I know and I certainly fall into this trait, we were 'good' players, but not necessarily 'great' players to where it came naturally to us. I think a lot of coaches appreciate coaching, because they needed coaching. I wasn't a 5-star recruit and the game didn't come simply to me based solely on athletic ability. And I think that's true for a lot of coaches. When you are coached like that, when you're a good not great player but you have the passion, you tend to appreciate the coaching; you appreciate the patience it takes and the teaching involved in making you a better football player. I didn't forget that in high school and in college it surely rang true.

I went to Springfield College, which basically produces nothing but coaches. But that's really the passion for the game, the passion for improvement, and I think one of the great things about coaching is that you have very tangible results. You can look and see did we get better? Did we win? But also when you break it down to an individual kid, is he improving? Is he doing what you're asking him to do? So, I knew fairly early on that coaching is what I wanted.

This is a game that you have to have a passion for in order to play. Lets face it…it hurts sometimes to play football! You have to have that passion that you enjoy every aspect of football. I tell the kids here at Colgate, you have to enjoy the process of winning football games. Everybody loves running out of the tunnel on a Friday or Saturday and wearing the uniform, getting the fanfare that comes with playing the game. But to me, the passion for football is that Tuesday practice, when it's a little cold and raining and you know you still have to work on whatever physical skill you need to work on, or compete in any drill that's being competed in on the practice field. I just have a ton of respect for people that have that passion, that understand that it's practice that's going to make Saturday go for us. I haven't lost that, and I try to instill that in our guys. When you get kids rallying and competing on a Tuesday afternoon and they're giving that maximum effort when they're still banged up from the Saturday before, you learn to cherish those moments. I've been doing this for 20 years, and there's still nothing like an inside run period to get my heart going! I just think that the level of commitment, and level of passion is what I love about football.

I want my impact to be that our teams played it the right way. We still value the core values of football which is, eleven working as one. Playing a physical brand of football, the way it's meant to be played. I think especially for me being at an academic institution, one of the things that I try to really instill in our players is don't be a stereotype. What I mean by that is, people make certain assumptions about football players and a lot of those are incorrect and misinformed. So, I try to teach my guys that you can be a dominant, physical football player on the field, and still be a great student, great person, great leader, great father and a great husband off the field. I think in our sport today, that's very important. There are a lot of people out there that just want to shoot down the behavior of football players, when 95% are great people that give a lot sacrifice to play this game. I want to be known as the guy that instills that but also appreciates that in football players.

JOEY JONES
HEAD COACH - UNIVERSITY OF SOUTH ALABAMA
WWW.USAJAGUARS.COM - @COACHJOEYJONES

I had somewhat of a rough childhood. My father died when I was young and there were a lot of things going on at the time with me personally. I started playing football at the age of seven and I just fell in love with it. I played a Maitre Park here in Mobile, AL. I had a coach that really took me under his wing and taught me mental toughness, how to play the game and I've just been in love with it ever since.

I loved playing the game. I played for 20 years, and once I was done, I had to really decide on what it was I wanted to do with my life. I tried the real estate business for about 6 months but I kept finding myself going to watch people practice and going to Friday night games in high school football; I just realized that this was in my blood and it's what I really enjoyed doing everyday, the being around the players and being a part of their life. So after that short amount of time, I realized that football is where I needed to be and what I needed to do.

I love the strategy of the game. One of my favorite days of the week is Sunday when you get the film, start to break down the opponent and try to figure out ways that you can win the football game. That's the most exciting part for me. Going through that process throughout the week, is what I love the most.

The one thing we talk about a lot with our players is that how much we want these guys to be warriors on the field, and gentlemen off the field; and I hope they remember that about me, and how I went about business. When we're in a ball game…it's on! But when we're off the field, we treat people with respect and caring about them. That's the twofold thing that I always tell my guys.

TROY CALHOUN
HEAD COACH - AIR FORCE ACADEMY
WWW.GOAIRFORCEFALCONS.COM - @COACHTCALHOUN

It's the ultimate team sport. So the bonds that you forge, the demands, the duress, the physical contact, the stamina, the kind of growth that occurs as a human being is truly what makes it such a remarkable game. It's not only your basic character traits that can be grasped and understood when you play the sport of football: courage, work ethic, unselfishness, humility, grit, respect for others, and being able to persevere. It's being able to push through when you are a little bit tired, sore, or go through some adversity.

The adrenaline of the competition certainly is something that stirs anybody that's a part of it. It's such a magnificent game that teaches so much; so many lessons like character and leadership that's carried forward when they are done playing. I always thought it was one of those sports that absolutely got in your blood in a hurry. I love all athletics. I was a three-sport athlete in high school, started in football, basketball and baseball. In football I was a quarterback, basketball I was a point guard and baseball I was a middle infielder and I'm a strong believer in good healthy competition. The friendships that you can make and the lifelong bonds and rapport that you develop with so many people that otherwise you may never have met and been able to interact if you were not involved in sports and specifically football.

I want to just be the vehicle, the avenue, the doors that football opened for those that were a part of it to earn an even better education, to grow as human beings and to develop the kind of souls or essence of who they are to make our communities stronger, to be very healthy contributing members to their own families and help those around them. I think football does a heck of a job teaching some of those key values and those principles.

BRANDON LONDON

RETIRED PRO FOOTBALL PLAYER

ACTOR/TV HOST/MODEL

Hands down, my father really drew me into the game of football. My father played college ball and was an undrafted free agent with the Dallas Cowboys and because of a knee injury, he couldn't play ball anymore, so he got into coaching. Football has been in my family since day 1. My uncle was a Division 1 athlete. He was drafted by the Seattle Mariners but went to college to play both football and baseball. Both, my dad and my uncle blew their knees out, so I wanted to be the one London to make it to the pros.

I think the competitive aspect of football is what kept me going. I come from a family of competitors, both my mom's and my dad's side of the family. I already mentioned that it was in my family from day 1, but now you add in the competing against others, the physical aspect of the game, and I'm not afraid to say it, but the shine of the game as well. I grew up liking guys like Deion Sanders and Michael Irvin. Watching those flashy type guys, I enjoyed the way they played ball and had a good time on the field. It was like being a showman out there. With my father being a coach, I got to see a lot of different guys and their path to try and make it to the NFL. I got to see how they worked; how they stayed late; how they worked out a lot. So me seeing that, I kind of put together my own little formula on how I was going to make it and it worked!

Now that I'm retired, I hope people would look back on my career and say that I was one of those solid players, who also had fun. I know I wasn't an NFL or CFL hall of famer, but I was a showman out there. I took advantage of the opportunities that the game awarded me. So, I want people to say that Brandon London was a smart man, who played some good football and was also very successful once his playing career was done.

BRANDON BOUTIN

PASTOR, MOTIVATIONAL SPEAKER - 2B MINISTRIES
WWW.2BMINISTRIES.COM - @BRANDONBOUTIN

Initially, what drew me into the game of football growing up was being around my family. The men in my family, aunts and uncles, virtually everybody was Saints fans. One day, I happened to walk into a room and I saw everyone cheering. They were cheering, screaming and hollering while watching this game called football. At that moment when I saw the effect it had on my family, how it literally had the ability to make everybody happy, make everybody feel good and had the ability to bring everybody together, it hit me…this is something I want to participate in. If I can participate in this, which is bringing a lot of people this much happiness, this is something I want to look into and be a part of. That was the initial thing to spark my interest in football. It was a game that had the ability to unify a group of people.

I love the fellowship, the brotherhood and the sense of family that comes with football. It was so unifying that you had all of these guys come together for a common goal, a common cause and that was to win. The goal was to win, to get better and in order to accomplish that, we had to work together; we had to work hard; we had to run, lift, we had to make sacrifices. So it was that fellowship and brotherhood that really stuck out to me about football, which made me fall in love with the game.

I want people to know how passionate I was about this game. I wanted people to feel my passion more than anything. If they saw my passion, they understood me. If they saw my passion, they understood why I worked that hard in the gym; why I wanted to bring it everyday at practice; why I put the time in and didn't mind staying after practice to work on my game. I didn't mind doing all of these things because I was that passionate about the game. Still to this day, I run into to people that know me, and they remember that passion and dedication I played with. And that passion that I had for football has carried over in my life to everything that I've done, and everything that I do.

I was a shy kid coming into football. There were a lot of things that I didn't know about myself. And the passion that I show now, I'd have to say that football brought that out of me. I've learned that football has the ability to bring out skills and talents in an individual that you don't know you possess. I didn't know that I had so much passion, until I was tested. I specifically remember when I realized this; it was back in junior high at McMain. Coach Sam Hill had us running laps around the school.

I remember at the time I was in 7th grade, guys were older than me and I couldn't keep up. But, instead of me saying 'I can't do it', there was something that sparked inside of me that made me says, "I'm going to finish... and one day, I'll finish first". It was at that moment the passion was sparked inside of me and created this desire to be the best at what I did. So, if it wasn't for the physical and mental challenges that football put me through, I don't believe I would have this passion today.

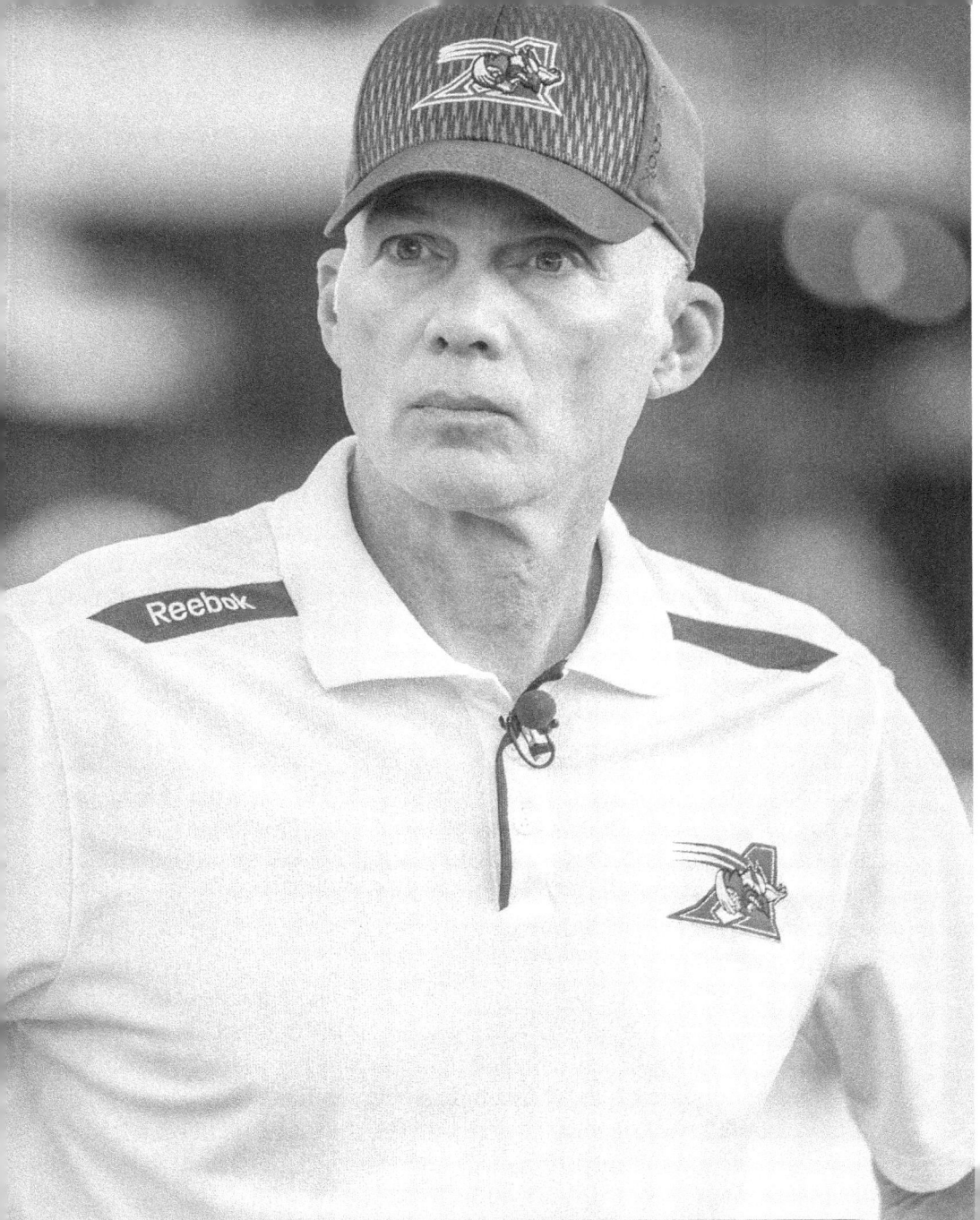

TOM HIGGINS
HEAD COACH - MONTREAL ALOUETTES
WWW.MONTREALALOUETTES.COM - @MTLALOUETTES

I think I was blessed to grow up in a football environment. My dad played at the University of North Carolina. He was there when Charlie "Choo-Choo" Justice was there. My dad ended up getting drafted by the Chicago Cardinals and played for the Philadelphia Eagles after that. I just grew up in a football environment. There wasn't a year that I can remember, where I wasn't involved in the sport. My dad went on to coach at two high schools: West Side High School in Newark, NJ and Piscataway High School in Piscataway, NJ; he spent almost 40 years as a high school football coach. I didn't know any different.

Football was always around. I remember when I wanted to start playing, which was about 6th grade; I had to plead with my dad to play. I don't know why he was holding me back, but he obviously wanted it to be my choice. What was interesting is that when I was with my dad, he would never give us a football to play with while he was coaching at the games, we had to bring our own. We would actually take rolls of tape and mold it into a football so that we would have something to play with. So with all of that going on, being around the game, to eventually playing it, I just kind of knew that this was the sport for me.

I don't think football ever 'leaves' an individual, I think they take something with them because of all of the things football teaches you. What's fascinating is that I knew in 9th grade that football was something I wanted to do for a living. I was still playing Pop Warner, and I remember you had to be 115lbs. I know I was between 115-140lbs at that time. My dad was a big man, so I always thought that I'll eventually grow, but I wanted to play professional football. I always thought that I'd play pro ball for 10 years…that obviously didn't happen, but I knew back then that I wanted football to be a big part of my life.

During that time, it was one of those things that many different people influence you in life. I think people get this in other sports, but particularly in football, gentlemen come into your life that, all of a sudden have a tremendous impact. They might not know that at the time. All of a sudden, football became what I wanted to do. I wanted to give back to the sport that gave me so much. You can only play the game for so long. I was very fortunate to go to North Carolina State and play for 4 years under Lou Holtz. He influenced me…as well as the other assistant coaches, but Coach Holtz had a big affect on me. So it was during this entire period of time that I knew football would be something that I'd pursue long term.

Football is the ultimate challenge. What it takes to succeed in football is exactly what it takes to succeed in life and in business. In football, you can do some things a lot better than any business can because of the evaluation process. There's so much that can be drawn from the game of football, and as I sit here today looking back, I have no regrets. I do tell a lot of young coaches that are getting into the profession, that this is the best and worst profession in the world. Worst in the sense that you usually don't have much control of the longevity of your tenure as a coach. If you look at a lot of coaches' resumes, they usually have multiple spots. It's not like corporate America where they can stay with the company for their entire career. But I do think a lot of coaches feel as though they've never worked a day in their life. Yeah, you put in a lot of hours, but the reward is something that is indescribable.

When you compete as an athlete, you go out on the field and perform to the best of your abilities, it doesn't guarantee that you're going to win because it's a team sport. Everyone is working together in order for you to have that euphoria of playing and finishing a game. It gets me excited even to this day. So when you coach, you don't physically get beat up anymore; you might mentally, but you still get the opportunity to experience the same feeling you did when you were a player. But the players that go out on the field, and I tell them all the time, are a reflection of the coaching staff. I take a lot of pride in what that reflection should look like. I do, and the players should also understand, that when you go out on that field, you're representing something bigger than yourself. The name that's on the back of your jersey, that's your family. The name that's on the front of your jersey, in this case it is Montreal, you're representing the city of Montreal, the province of Quebec and the country of Canada. So, all of those things kind of tie into one another and for me, that's the real thrill.

I don't know if I'd want my imprint to be on the game more so than the players I had the pleasure of working with. I think you leave a little bit behind with every player. Having an opportunity to reflect back because I started at a young age on the professional level coaching, it's when you see a lot of the older players you've coached come back and say 'thank you what an impact you had on my life.' Those are the moments that remind you why you do what you do.

CHRIS PALMER

SENIOR OFFENSIVE ASSISTANT - BUFFALO BILLS
WWW.BUFFALOBILLS.COM - @BUFFALOBILLS

Like a lot of kids I played three sports in high school. I enjoyed basketball the most and was probably the best at baseball but football was a sport I wanted to coach because of the strategy involved. I was fortunate to get into it right after college. I stayed involved in the game despite not being able to compete as a player anymore but I was able to compete as a coach. I went into it not knowing if it was going to be a long time. I've been fortunate; this is my 33rd year of coaching. In the back of my mind I realized there were only so many jobs and if it didn't work out I would've had to move on to support my family.

I enjoy being around the players. Players need coaches and coaches need players. The other night I went out to dinner with a guy that played for me 35 years ago and that relationship continues to develop even after their done playing. Those are the things that are rewarding.

CHARLIE COINER
FOUNDER - 1ST DOWN TECHNOLOGIES LLC
FORMER COLLEGE & NFL COACH
WWW.FIRSTDOWNPLAYBOOK.COM

Like a lot of people, my dad got me into football. My dad was a sports fan, a Green Bay Packer fan, a Bear Bryant fan and that's what got me started. You can't help it when your dad is that passionate about it. Not only the football part, he was a big military guy that really preached hard work and discipline. He would point out those things he saw on the field and the things that [Vince] Lombardi or [Bear] Bryant would say. That's where it started. If my dad wasn't as big of a football player as he was, I might not be doing what I'm doing right now.

I never played college football, which is the unique thing about my situation. I was from a small town and at the time I thought I was a very good baseball player, but as it turns out, I was an okay baseball player. I went to Catawba College and probably could've done better but like a lot of kids I made really poor decisions. I tried to focus on one thing when I went to college, but to answer your question, at the age of 15 I thought I would be a football coach. I had the initial influence of my father, but I was very fortunate to have a strong leadership figure in my high school football coach as well. I looked at him and he was everything my father was with the passion part of it, but he actually knew what he was talking about. He understood and taught me football as much as you could at the high school level. He was also my baseball coach. I remember distinctly him looking at us in a classroom asking, 'What do you want to do when you grow up?' I looked right at him and said, 'I want your job.' That's why not playing college football wasn't as big of a deal to me. I wanted to but I thought I might be a professional baseball player, I thought I would eventually become a high school football coach. I had no idea I would coach in college. I knew I wasn't big enough or fast enough to be a great football player so I wasn't going to play big time college football, but I thought I could coach since the age of 15.

I don't think that there's any game like football. I've been involved in athletics my whole life. There was never a sport to me that required a person doing his own job and having 11 different people doing their own job and it all had to have a variant scheme. As a young athlete you don't truly get everything, but you can see where there's a whole lot more work going into it. To me there is no other game that combines strategy and individual techniques that come together with combination techniques. If you take the cornerbacks in high school, he probably can't tell you what the left guard or left tackle are doing on a play and if you take the right guard, he can't tell you what the wide receiver is doing.

They're responsible for their area. But as a coach you're responsible for knowing the whole thing and seeing the beauty of the game and how it ties in together. All of those things I loved from a strategic point. It also goes back to my dad and the discipline he taught me. My coaches also taught me that if I worked hard, I had a chance to be successful. That's why I had a chance to be on a successful high school football team and it really made an impression on me. The work ethic I gained from football is why I believe there isn't anything like it. I agree that we have to continue to make our game better, but I don't believe there are enough people talking about all the good things football does for people.

I hope that anyone that played for me in college or in the NFL would say that he is very organized, a great teacher and always looked to make players better; a lot of times that might mean helping guys off of the field. I'd like for people to say he always made it about the players and it was never about himself. In today's coaching world where everyone wants to move up the ranks, I never did so at the expense of the players.

MIKE SINGLETARY
PRO FOOTBALL HALL OF FAME LINEBACKER
FORMER NFL HEAD COACH & ASSISTANT COACH

I knew football was something I wanted to do from a very young age. From playing touch football in the street or tackle football on the gravel, I knew I loved the game. It was a great outlet for me because, having grown up in a single-parent home, it was a great way to develop as a young man. It kept me out of trouble, set boundaries for me and the Lord led me to some great men…it just happened to be coaches!

The year my brother passed away and my mom and dad divorced, was when football brought clarity to me. My mom told me that she needed me to step up and be the man of the house. I went into my room and wrote out my vision statement. My vision statement was to get a scholarship to college, become an All-American in college, get my college degree, get drafted and go to the NFL, ultimately to buy my mother a house and take care of her for the rest of my life. I also wrote that I wanted to become an All-Pro and own my own business. So when I was 12 years old when my brother passed away and the divorcing of my parents, football brought that much needed clarity.

I'll let God decide what my football legacy will be. I'm in a place right now where I know he has an 'end' but, I'm excited to see what he writes!

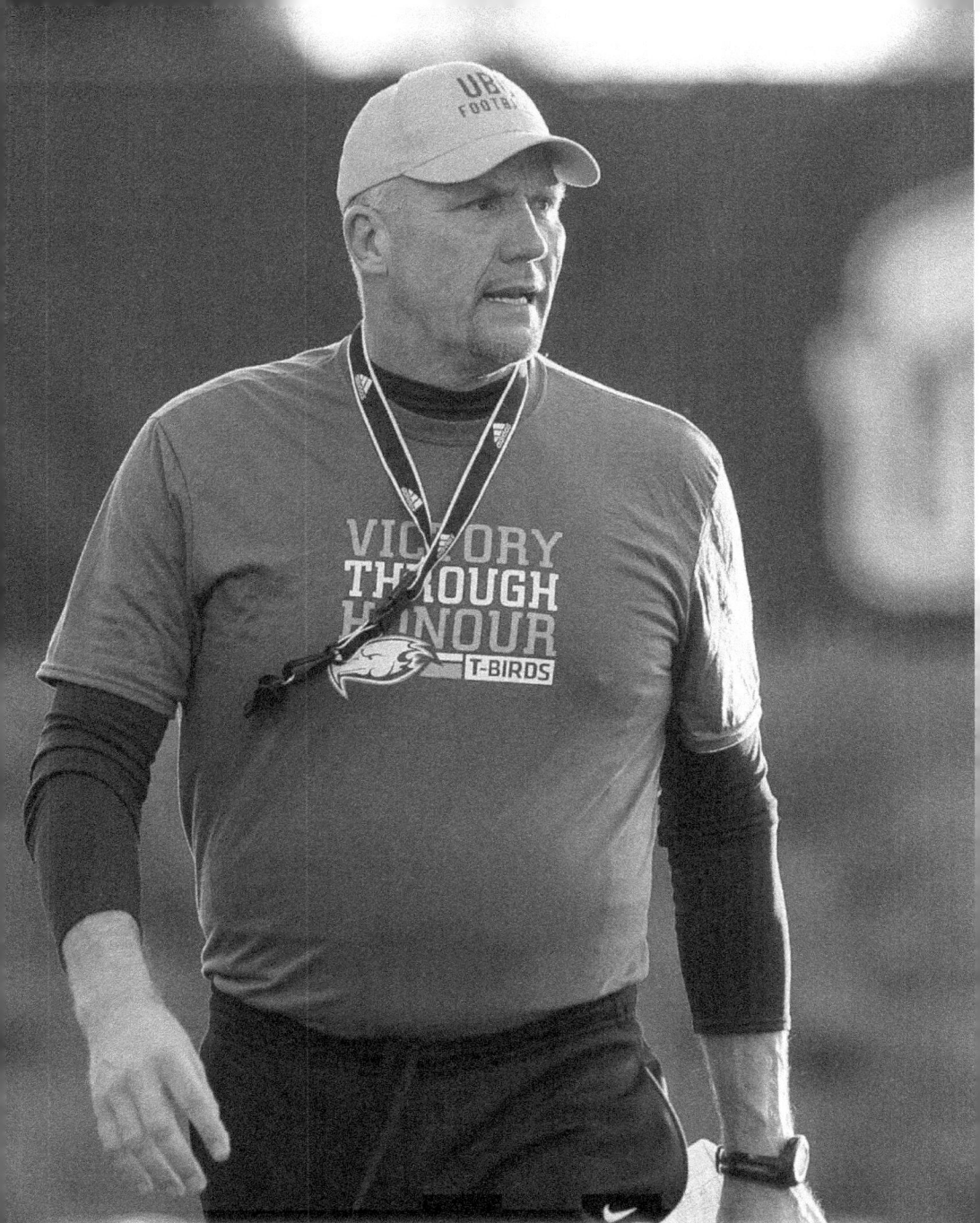

BLAKE NILL

HEAD COACH - UNIVERSITY OF BRITISH COLUMBIA
WWW.GOTHUNDERBIRDS.CA - @UBCTBIRDS

I started football very late. I came from an agriculture background, so I walked-on at the university and that was my first time playing football. I had not played organized football prior to that. What I was always intrigued about was the raw enthusiasm associated with the game. Being in the crowd as a young kid or teenager, it was just the energy associated with the game, both on and off the field, I thought was incredible.

I think what happened at the university level, I realized that not only did I 'want it', but about 100-110 young men at each program that 'wanted it' as well. So you quickly learn to compete within your program and you have to find a way to separate yourself from everyone else, in order to gain reps and playing time with the hopes of catching the attention of someone who thinks you have the potential of being a pro. Initially in my college career, it was a wake up call that told me 'hey, you're not alone in this pursuit of a professional goal'; so if you can develop a competitive mindset, you may have a chance.

The passion you see from both players and coaches is unlike any other sport. Everyone who participates in sports is passionate about their sport, but football is different. It's an ultimate team game. It's a game where your success relies on the other 11 or as in the U.S., the other 10 guys on the field. So consequently, you develop a trust issue and you develop a mindset that you can't let your teammates down. Those skillsets are transitioned into your adult life and into the career stage of your life. That's why so many football players are so successful at the career stage of their life beyond football. I was just so impressed as a young man by the teamwork involved with football and now as a man that's coached football for almost 25 years, I'm able to tell my players that this is the benefit of playing this game, if you approach the game correctly.

PETE SHINNICK

HEAD COACH - UNIVERSITY OF WEST FLORIDA

WWW.GOARGOS.COM - @PETESHINNICK

I grew up around the game of football. My dad played in the NFL and coached in the NFL, so I was always around the game; and I just LOVED being a part of it. So it was a very, very simple transition for me to go from watching, to playing. I would have to say that it was during college when I realized that I wanted football to be my career. I was getting a business degree and I did a couple of internships, a couple of summer jobs and I was working in sales, I was working in marketing; and I came to the realization that this was not for me. I did not want to spend my life behind a desk. I needed to be out; I needed to be involved with people more; I needed to feel like I was teaching and encouraging. So it was at that time that I was like 'alright, how do you get into college coaching and what does that look like?'

Football parallels life. There are many ups and downs, there's hard work, there's discipline that needs to be involved in order to succeed. Seventy years down the line, I just hope that I was known to be a guy that cared about the people that played for him and one that had a positive impact on them.

DENAULD BROWN
Head Coach - Munich Cowboys (Germany)
www.munich-cowboys.de - @MunichCowboys

I was the youngest of three children growing up and sports were a big part of our lives. My brother and sister both ran track. We were living in Florida and my birthday fell at a time where I couldn't play football. And my mom didn't want me to play anyway. I ended up playing baseball as my first sport. So I was one of those late starters, as my mom didn't let me play football until I was in junior high school and I was 12 years old. So, I guess what really drew me into football was curiosity. I played every other sport but football and wanted to see what it was about. In 6th grade, my first experience playing the game, I took to it like a fish to water and didn't look back. I was naturally good at it, and it allowed me to basically express myself in a way that I never could before. I wasn't a very good communicator when I was young. I was very shy and football allowed me to express myself without having to verbalize. Me moving to Pennsylvania at the time, it was like the universe brought football to me, rather than me going to it.

I sort of grew into wanting football to be my career. Not everyone can grow to be 6'4. I was tall, fast and had a lot of physical tools. People looked at me and said 'wow, you're a big dude.' In baseball, I was stealing bases like I was small. I was very fast for my size. In between my 8th grade year and my freshman year in high school, I went from 5'11 to 6'3 ½. When people started confirming to me how good I was, because I didn't know how good I was, I knew then that I wanted to do this for the rest of my life.

Football is a snapshot of life. You have an advantage playing football; you're able to learn life lessons in the microcosm of a game that allows you to sort of vet life during that time. You begin to realize by having that advantage of being in situations on the field with your teammates, adverse situations, and team situations, to where you make it about them and not yourself, to me that's a benefit. And that's something you can't ever take back. Football gave me everything. It gave me a career. It gave me a chance to travel all over the world. That to me, has always been the one thing about football that you can't take away. It is also, the one thing about the game that I really love. The fact of the matter is that when I think back to being that 12 year old starting football, there's no way I could've ever imagined I'd be coaching football in Germany as an adult.

I'll be 40 years old this year, so time is flying by. I'm at the age right now where you'll go to the AFCA convention and see guys that you've coached. At that point, you begin to realize how much you really influence people. That takes time. You won't know that for years. So when a player calls or emails you years later and says 'thanks coach, you influenced me.' It makes you sit back and say wow; I was able to affect this young man. I recruited him, brought him to a school, I saw him grow from a young man to a man, and now he's gone off and has his own thing going and his own family. That to me, is the type of legacy I want to leave. It's really a small victory for me because it's not like my impact would be world known. That's a story that virtually every coach has. As a matter of fact, coaches who coached me have told that same story. Now I know what they feel. Football is just an endless cycle of opportunities. So, I would like to think my legacy would be giving players the opportunity to be successful by coaching them they way they're supposed to be coached.

KEVIN RAMSEY

DEFENSIVE COORDINATOR - ALABAMA STATE UNIVERSITY
WWW.BAMASTATESPORTS.COM - @ASUBUZZ

My love for the game came at an early age. I'm a product of the sixties, I grew up in East St. Louis and I can close my eyes right now and hear the sounds of the neighborhood. I can hear the girls' double-dutching. I can see down the streets people hop-scotching; drawing all over the streets and on the sidewalks. So in my neighborhood, I had my 'team' when I was about 12 or 13 years old, we would line up and run pass routes or play in the backyard of my friend who lived three blocks away from me, so just that love for the game started very early for me emulating coaches. So early on, coaching had a real profound effect on me…there was even a future Butkus Award winner on my 'team' in Dana Howard, who grew up right across the street from me.

Man, I've been so blessed. I played for one of the most legendary high school coaches in all of America in Bob Shannon. He had a profound effect on me and not just him, but also the coaches he surrounded himself with too. To be able to go through his football program, teaching the discipline and why you need desire to play this game, meant a great deal. He always had a lot of hope for me. He expected me to do certain things and desired for me to do certain things and it made me into the person that I am today.

I hope that the players I coached are able to say that I expected the best out of them and desired the best from them as well.

BRAD BUSTLE

OFFENSIVE LINE COACH - CUMBERLAND UNIVERSITY

WWW.GOCUMBERLANDATHLETICS.COM - @COACHBUSTLEB

For me, it was just growing up around my dad. He was a big time college football coach. At the time I was born, he was coaching at Virginia Tech. When I really started understanding football, and being around it, they (Virginia Tech) were pretty successful. Being around him, being around the players and basically growing up around those guys, being out there at practice everyday and going to my dad's office everyday, is what really initially drew me into the game of football. So in my mind as a kid, I thought I'd just grow up, be a college football player and go to bowl games because it looks easy!

I want to say moving from Virginia to Louisiana made me want to be involved in the game so much more. Going to the Deep South where football is this very important thing, more so than where I grew up, you had to work so hard just to play in high school. I get down to Louisiana and the kids are bigger, stronger and faster than anything I've ever seen. So, I went to thinking 'I don't know if this is for me.' I was nervous, intimidated and ended up not playing one season. But at that point, I made up my mind to do this, to put the work in, give it everything I've got, and see it through. I started growing into my body more. I worked out really hard in the weight room and I just saw the improvements that I was making through hard work; and this was probably one of the first times in my life that I've put this much effort into something. Now, all of a sudden, you become a part of this team, this family and you have that drawing you into it more as well. Now it went from a school that has 60-70 players on a team, to now having 60-70 of your brothers on the team. You're going through the same things, having the same experiences; working toward the same goals and that captured me once I was mature enough to understand that. My senior year in high school, I was playing really well, started winning awards and that's when I started thinking 'hey, I may be able to do this in college.' That's when it sort of became a reality for me that I might just be able to do this long term.

What I love about the game, and football individually over any other sport the most is that every person's responsibility is equal to every other person's responsibility if you want success. From a coach's perspective, it's amazing to see how important every little detail is at every position on the field. If one guy messes up, that whole play can be botched. I played left guard, and my offensive line coach would say 'you want to put your worst offensive lineman at left guard' (laughs), so that was me! In all seriousness, he said that because you have a little bit more room for error at that position.

But at the same time, if I made a mistake, the whole play would be screwed up. Football is such a team sport in comparison to other sports and that's what I love about it the most. If you have 9 or 11 coaches, depending on where you're at, they have to do their job equally or things won't work. If I'm coaching the heck out of my offensive line, or the receivers coach is coaching the heck out of his wide receivers and I'm not doing my job with the offensive line, then we won't have a good team.

When I first started coaching football, I realized I could be pretty good at it. And I think I had the mindset of every young coach where I want to go and become this big-time offensive coordinator or head coach; thinking I want to have the best offense in the nation or the best defense in the nation if I were a defensive coordinator; thinking that I want to have the best team in the nation, coach on the big stage and win a bunch of bowl games. That was sort of my mindset in the beginning and I was going to do whatever it took to get there. But, I think that has changed a lot since I've been here at Cumberland University.

Being at a smaller school, I realized that I just really enjoy what I'm doing. The players that I coach, and have coached, mean a lot to me. I don't look at it as a stepping-stone as much anymore. I literally have 20 players in my room that I'm going to have an impact on their lives. They've had elementary, middle and high school teachers that have taught them all of these lessons, and I'm kind of the final teacher/mentor/coach that they're going to be around before they step into the real world. And it dawned on me these last couple of years that it is the type of impact I can have on each individual player. So when I'm done coaching, I want know that I gave each and every last one of my players, my 100% effort and tried to not only help them become better players, but become better people. I know it's very cliché but, you've become so close to these guys and you realize how much of an impact you really have on these guys and then it dawns on you that 'shoot…this is real.' The feeling of wanting them to be better people and making them be better people going forward, is a real feeling. And it's a real motivation that you end up having.

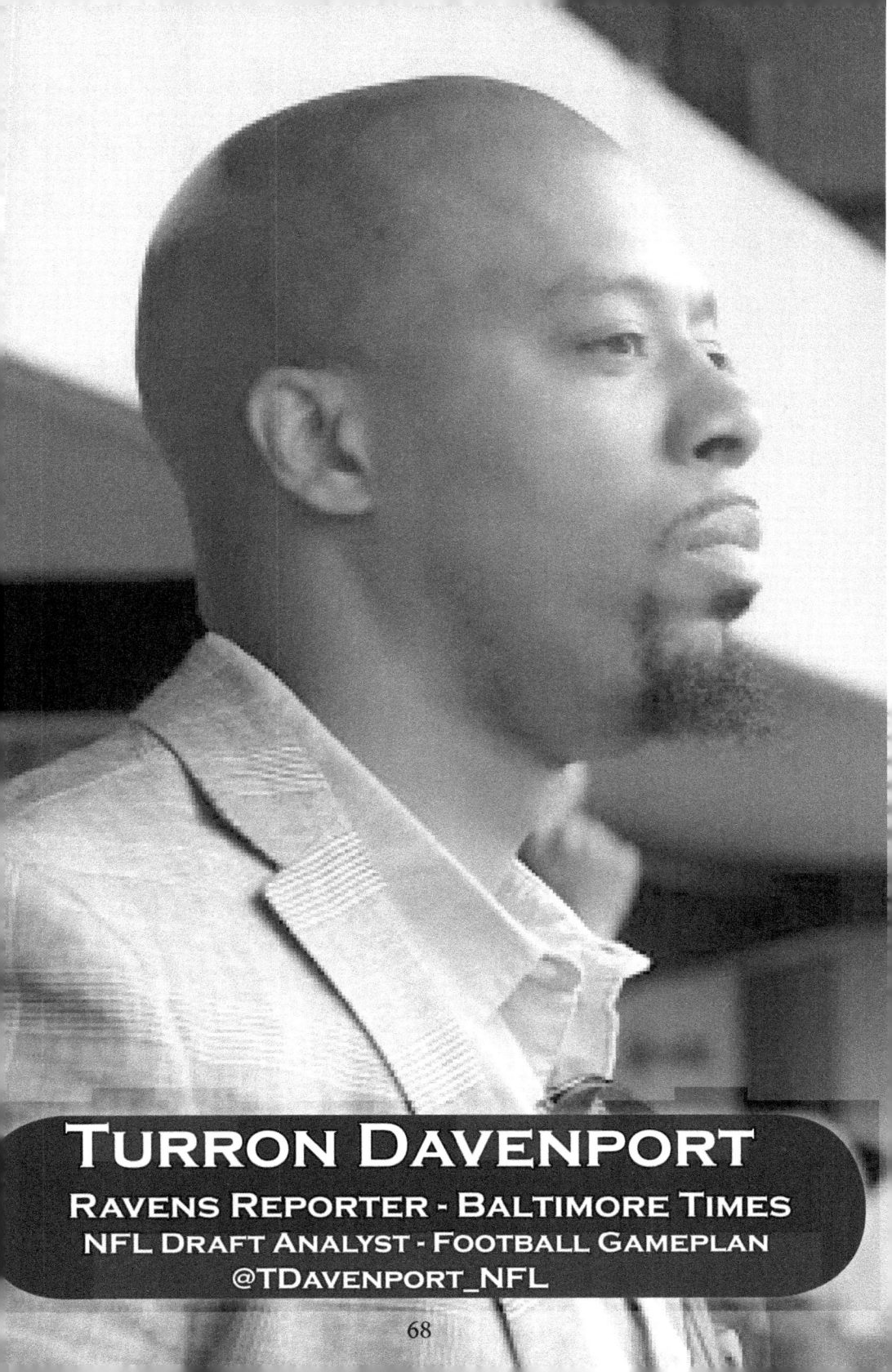

TURRON DAVENPORT

RAVENS REPORTER - BALTIMORE TIMES
NFL DRAFT ANALYST - FOOTBALL GAMEPLAN
@TDavenport_NFL

The thing that I love most about football is the competition and the attention that it garners. There is no better feeling than beating your man in one-on-one coverage on a route and making the big catch. You get up, look into the stands and see all eyes on you. It's addictive. It doesn't matter if there are 1,000 or 100,000 people in the stands. It's like the Tupac song, "All Eyez On Me." That is the feeling.

I love getting the chance to prepare for an opponent and having it pay off when we engage in competition. Football is a series of small competitions. Going out on the field and playing football on gameday is a reward for all of the hard work that was put into practice. Even in practice, you compete for the opportunity to play in the games. The coaches' eyes are on you and it is up to you to do everything that you can to make him afraid to not let you play.

The beauty of competition is that it can happen among friends or foes. As receivers, we used to compete to see who could have the most catches or who could make the most outstanding catch. It drives you to raise your game to the next level and do things that you may not normally be capable of. The feeling that you get when a teammate comes up to you and says; "Man, that was a nice play!" is addictive.

When you step onto the field, the person on the opposite side of the ball is a foe. It's a privilege to get to compete. It's a clash of wills. He wants to keep you from catching the ball, and in your mind, you HAVE to catch the ball. Who is going to win?

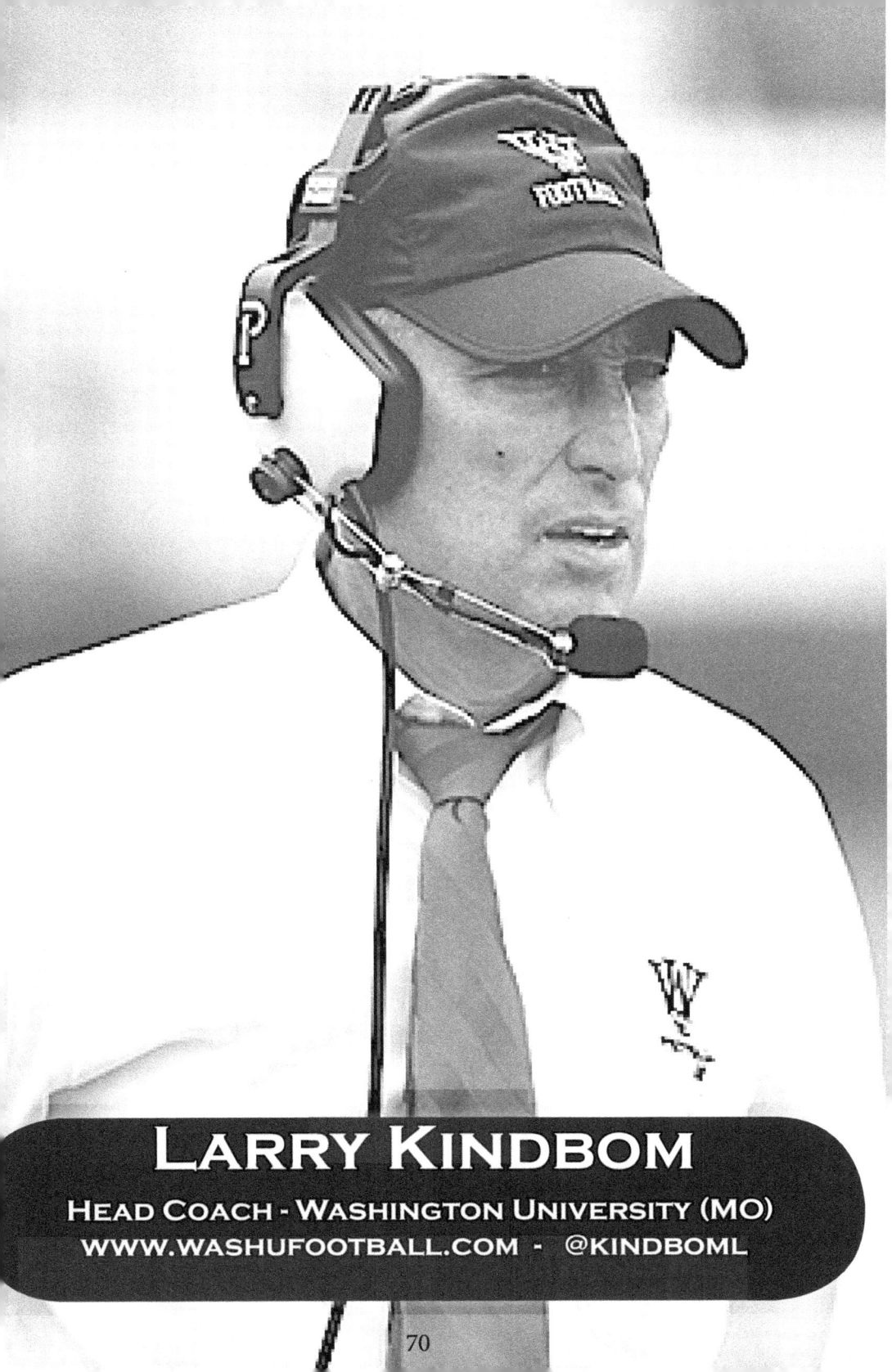

LARRY KINDBOM

HEAD COACH - WASHINGTON UNIVERSITY (MO)
WWW.WASHUFOOTBALL.COM - @KINDBOML

What initially drew me into the game of football was the fact that it was just and fair. When I went to high school, I weighed 117lbs my sophomore year. I went out for wide receiver; I'd been a quarterback up until that point. And the wide receiver position at my high school was a position to where you lined up 6 inches away from the tight end. We didn't have a 'wide' wide receiver, which is what I wanted to be. I was lined up with three other guys at my position, two of which ended up playing in the Ivy League. And at that time, both were big animals, they were 220-225lbs, so they were big men back then. This was back in 1967. So on the first day, after we finished our stretching, coach blows the whistle to gather everybody up and he has 2 dummies on the ground. He's screaming out names and mine one was one of the two he called out. So as we're running up, I had no idea what this was, but the other guy was already down in his stance and he's trying to explain to me quickly what was essentially the "Oklahoma Drill". I didn't know what it was, never seen it.

So at this point, I have absolutely no idea what's going on. All of a sudden the whistle blows and I'm lying on my back. So, he runs me over and tackles the ball carrier. Everyone is cheering and yelling as they pull guys off the pile. And while all of this is going on, I'm still on the ground and the offensive line coach stands over me and screams "Get Up Kindbom! We NEVER lay on the ground". That was my first experience with high school football. I've never experienced anything like that and that's the way we started practice everyday. So fast forward to the middle of October and we're back doing the Oklahoma Drill and now I'm on the defensive side of the ball and the same guy is now on the offensive side. Next thing you know, the running back fall over this small pile that I created and the team is pulling me off the pile by my feet and cheering for me. I still remember looking back and there was our Offensive Line coach now standing over the other guy saying "Get Up, Get Up! We never lay on the ground". It was something just about that moment, which had me hooked on the game of football. I played sports all the way up through that point, but I never really felt that feeling I had right then and there. I was never getting yelled at because of my effort, but it was the fact that you never lay on the ground. I just didn't find that in other parts of my life where things came down to talent, ability or size, but it was just flat out do the best you can do.

The result part of it was the most important thing. Coach wasn't attacking my character, or telling me I was a bad football player, but instead telling me that if you get knocked on your rear end, you get right back up and compete. And I look back now, and here I am, doing this for a living. Going back to when I was 8 years old, I've been involved with football for 55 years now and there's still nothing like it! And the Oklahoma Drill is one of the drills I cherish as a coach because, in my opinion, it's what football is all about.

For me, it's the camaraderie that I love the most about football. Don't get me wrong, I love the intensity, the hitting, the speed of the game, the skill, the artwork that skill guys use and the grind that the big guys use, but ultimately, I just love the camaraderie. The fact that you get two groups of people, competing in a very violent game, yet to know that there is some justice to it. And I just love the camaraderie of how people come together, learn to be part of a team, pick each other up and move forward.
I want my players to say that I cared about them. That would be the greatest compliment to me that they knew that I cared. That just covers a lot of territory in a lot of ways. I was fortunate enough coach with the great Woody Hayes who would always say, "I'm not the smartest guy…BUT". Jim Dennison who would always say, "Well we don't have the best skill players out there…BUT". And all of those 'buts' came back to the fact that they were some how in their own way as coaches saying that, they have kids that care about each other and I hope that's a reflection of me. Ultimately, that is the greatest compliment that nay player could give me is that 'coach, I know you cared'.

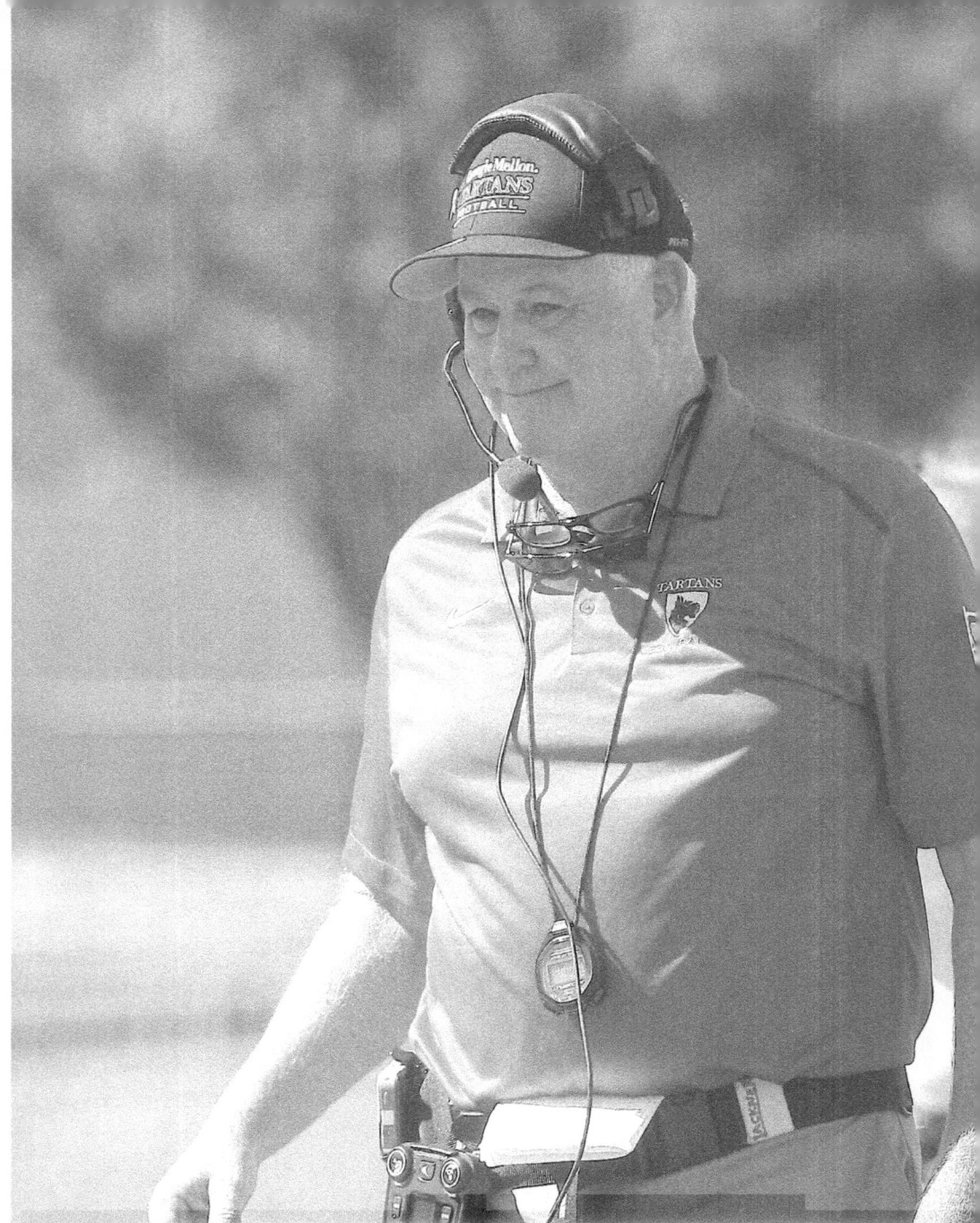

RICH LACKNER

HEAD COACH - CARNEGIE MELLON UNIVERSIT

WWW.ATHLETICS.CMU.EDU - @TARTANATHLETICS

As a young man, I was always involved in sports. I'm one of five children; four of us were boys and it was a lot of competiveness right within our own household in terms of sports. In terms of football, I would have to say that I was blessed with really fine coaching. My high school coach, Art Walker, was a legend in western Pennsylvania. Then I was able to play, as a freshman at Carnegie-Mellon, for a guy by the name of Joseph Gasparella who played at Notre Dame and was a great man. And my final 3 years of playing, and first 7 years of coaching, I was fortunate to play for and coach under a guy by the name of Chuck Klausing who's in the College Football Hall of Fame. So, I think those guys had a great influence on me, to want to make a career in the game of football.

When I went to Carnegie Mellon, I studied history, I was involved with the education program and I always felt my calling was to work with young men. So, I got my degree in Education and had every intention of going to teach high school history and coaching football until Coach Klausing asked me to stay on as an assistant coach right after graduation. I know those things don't typically happen today; usually young coaches have to go through the whole GA (graduate assistant) process, interning process before they get their first coaching opportunity. I got mine directly out of college, so I was blessed in that way.

The game really hasn't changed over the years. What I really love the most is interacting with young people. I always tell people that I'm currently 58 years old; I'll be 59 in July, but when I wake up in August and it's time for fall camp, I'm suddenly a 19 or 20 year old again. How blessed can you be to go to work everyday and work with really great young men? Here at Carnegie Mellon, they truly epitomize the term "Student-Athlete." I'm very blessed to work with young men who are gifted academically, incredibly driven, motivated, focused, and determined. How much fun is that, you know?? I get in the huddle with them, look them in the eye and say 'Hey, can you believe they pay me to do this??' You talk about having a great job, I tell you, what I do for a living is a blessing.

Looking back as a coach, I would hope my players looked back and say that I was fair, honest and gave everybody an opportunity. Also, I like to think I made the game fun. I think some coaches take the fun out of the game of football when they get to the college level.

There's so much pressure on coaches today. It is probably less pressure at the Division III level. There is a push on coaches to win, win, win and I love to win as much as anybody, but I would hope my players can look back and say that we made it fun for them. I would hope they would think of me more than just a coach. I truly enjoy getting involved with helping them with internships, job opportunities and meeting alumni. So I just hope they're able to say that I gave back to them as much as they gave to Carnegie Mellon football. I feel like my coaching style is a two-way street. It's hard for me to look them in the eye and ask for their best, if I'm not giving them my best everywhere else.

JEFFREY SIMS

HEAD COACH - GARDEN CITY C.C.
WWW.GCCCKS.EDU - @COACHJSIMS

For me, I always wanted to play football because my dad played. I always asked to play when I was young. They would tell me to play soccer because they said that I was too small to play football. That made me want to play football more because football, is a sport where you can prove yourself. You can prove that you are big enough, strong enough or fast enough. There's always some spot that you can play. You could play receiver, quarterback or running back and if you couldn't play offense, then you can play defense. It was the sport that the neighborhood played. You go outside and they were playing ball.

I grew up in a single parent household. My dad was imprisoned when I was in college playing football. No one in my family had graduated from college. When I grew up, a lot of people didn't go to college; they just went to work. I went to college to play football. I didn't go to college to get an education. When I was in college, my football coach was the first person in my life to tell me that I should graduate from college. It was an expectation from him. People at home were just happy that I went to college. That's the case a lot of times. People are happy that you go to college. Going to college is not an accomplishment but competing in college is. My coach had positive expectations. He treated me as if I was going to graduate and that's what he expected from me. It's good to be around people who see you as a successful person. I believe that is how college football coaches see players or else they wouldn't invest so much time to set up the structures that they do. I really love the relationships you develop from football. It's the largest sport, so you have so many different types of people. It's cool to see a guy come in as a freshman, scared and never been away from home. I've seen guys go to their first restaurant before, then years later, you see them with their wife and kids with a job and being successful.

I think junior college football should grow, have more respect, and be in more cities than small towns. Right now, junior college football is one of the most polished brands that we have. There's a segment of our population that can't get into school because a lot of division I schools are making admissions so high. Junior college is open enrollment so you get a chance to come in and develop and earn the opportunity either athletically or academically. Junior college gives players an opportunity that they may not have had prior. I don't think it's fair if you decide whether or not a kid can be a football player because of something that they did as a sophomore. One of my goals in life is to start a junior college football in St. Louis. There should be a junior college team in every major city. You use football as a vehicle to education.

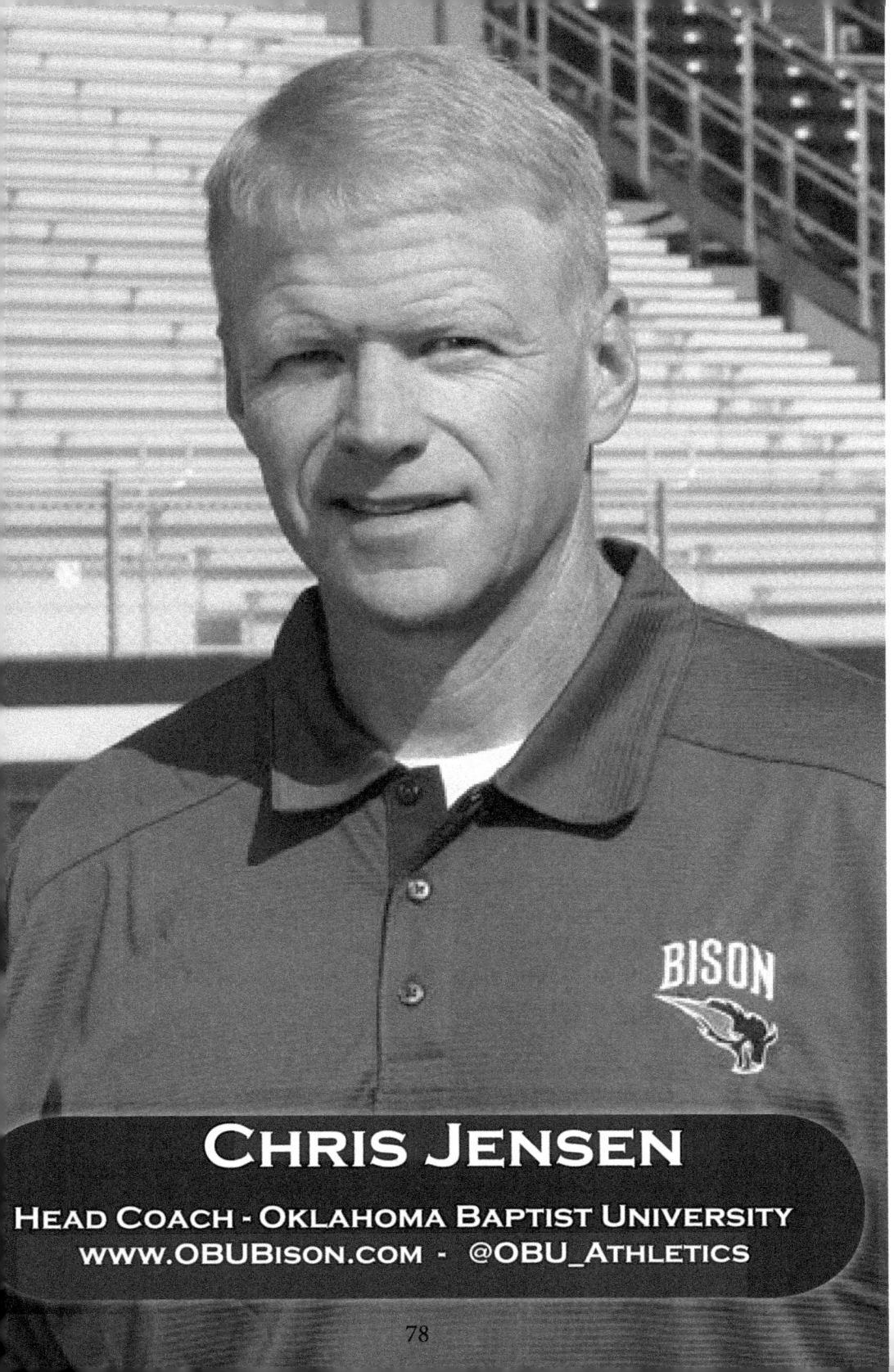

CHRIS JENSEN

HEAD COACH - OKLAHOMA BAPTIST UNIVERSITY
WWW.OBUBISON.COM - @OBU_ATHLETICS

I was in kind of a unique situation. I grew up in a military family; my dad was in the Army so we moved around a little bit. We lived in Germany for 3 years, and I wasn't really interested in sports, I mean…I played sports, but wasn't a diehard sports fan like a lot of guys that I know or like a lot of coaches I work with that grew up diehard fans. Especially in Oklahoma with the Sooner fans…and I just wasn't like that. My passion for the game didn't really develop until I was a junior, or senior in high school. Even though I played for a number of years, my passion of the game, in the sense of becoming a fan, didn't really develop until late.

For me, I started out in college as a business major. I thought I wanted to do that my first semester as I took economics, accounting and didn't go to class much. After that, I decided to change my major, did some soul searching and decided that football is something that I really enjoyed. And I didn't change my major until I was a junior in college, so I wasn't one of those guys that grew up wanting to coach my whole life. It was something that sort of developed in me throughout my college years. I also had to re-evaluate whether or not I wanted to make a whole lot of money in the profession. At the time, I went into public education and I coached at the high school level for 19 or 20 years before I got the job at Oklahoma Baptist. So, money wasn't that big of a deal, more so than having an impact on kids lives. That became more important.

What I love most about the game of football is how everything comes together. We can spend a lot of time on the whiteboard drawing up X's and O's, but when you can coach up the kids that you're working with, and you take that plan from the board, and see it executed on the field, that brings you a great deal of satisfaction. When things fit and happens the right way, that's brings the most joy. And you always have things that don't work out on the field, you go back to the drawing board and you keep going over and over it again…it just never stops!

I think the most important thing for me is that I had a godly influence on the kids that I'm working with. I feel like even more than a coach, I think my identity is in Christ. I pray that's what my players see. Whether or not they agree with my convictions at this point, at some point they realize and appreciate what I tried to do with them as players and as individuals. I really have reached a point in my life and in my career that X's and O's, wins and losses, they're important, but having an internal impact or a lasting impact on a kid is most important. I just pray that I can have that type of impact on the kids I've coached.

AARON KELTON
HEAD COACH - WILLIAMS COLLEGE
WWW.EPHSPORTS.WILLIAMS.EDU - @EPHSPORTS

The competitive edge and the physicality of the game is what drew me in. I grew up in an inner city environment where we were aggressive all the time. Growing up seeing the high school and semi-pro games made it very interesting. It's an easy game to play. All you need is a ball and two to three people. That's something that drew my brothers and me to the game because three of us could always just go outside and play. It was before high school for me when I realized that football is what I wanted to do long term. It was the fun times we had playing pop warner and before we got to high school. It was really just a fun time. The coaches made it fun. It was great being around those guys and I still have some of those friends from my pop warner football days. At that point I knew I really wanted to play and it was just reinforced by being on good teams and playing with guys and for coaches that cared for the players.

There are so many aspects about the game that I love. I love the competiveness, the X's and O's both as a player and a coach as well as the camaraderie that you have. I tell my team all the time here at Williams that there aren't many guys that go on to play in college. You're very fortunate and lucky so never embarrass the game. Always work hard to lift the game and never embarrass it. We all know that one guy who was great in high school and never went on to play in college or got injured in high school and couldn't play anymore. We're lucky that we were able to do that. But it's the fanfare, camaraderie, competitive edge, physicality of the game and the fun spirit that's with the game and behind the game. All those things make the game tremendous.

On being remembered, I'd say that not only I did it the right way, but also that I was able to create an opportunity for young men. I want them to think outside of the wins and losses and say Coach Kelton had a tremendous impact on me not just as a football player but also as a young man and as a person. If it's just one thing that I say that makes them better or makes them think about how lucky they are to have the experiences that they've had, then that's special.

BERT WILLIAMS

HEAD COACH - GEORGIA MILITARY COLLEGE

WWW.GMC.EDU - @GMCJCFBALL

As a young man, I played the game for as long as I could remember. It is what we did. We played it in the streets and in the yard. Football was something that was always just a part of the house. It wasn't until I was already in it that I realized that. I had a tough situation with my younger brother, it was just the two of us and he had a lifelong cardiac issue that went south quickly during my senior year of college. I was already accepted into the master's program at the University of Georgia. I was going to be a college professor. He was sent to a center at the University of Pittsburgh medical center. My dad was working on his startup business and I was looking for a way to pay my way through grad school. A friend of a friend told me that the University of Georgia had some openings for graduate assistants.

I enjoyed football; I loved the game so I figured that I would enjoy coaching. It was early but I wanted to pay for grad school because I was late in the process of applying. I didn't get any of the TA positions to help pay for it. We were trying to find a way to pay bills for my brother and I didn't want to be a burden on my family financially. Coach Ray Goff gave me the opportunity to coach and I enjoyed it.

A lot of the things that applied to coaching used to apply to the playing side. No matter who you are, where you're from what you're doing, you're going to be held accountable. Whatever you're accountable for, you'll be held to it. If you succeed you'll move forward. If you don't, coach said he just fine your ass! I just had to use my mind a little bit more. Use some of the lessons that I learned a little bit more. I always wanted to be a teacher. That is what coaching is. You teach different things. It's more emotional and can be more life influencing.

Football is the most democratic situation in the world today. Everyone has a helmet, shoulder pads and if you're not strong enough, hit the weight room, if you're not fast enough, run. Lose some weight and do what it takes. You have a chance to compete. Everyone plays by the same rules, has the same boundaries. It's a chance to compete and show that you're better than the guy in front of you. I enjoy doing that, even on a daily basis. I love practice, especially when you go out there and get after it and challenge each other.

I would like my players to say that I helped them to be a better player and person. If you could do those two things as a coach, you're doing everything that you could to help them to develop. It's about influencing them and developing them into the men that they can be. It's an awesome responsibility.

KEVIN GUY

HEAD COACH/GENERAL MANAGER - ARIZONA RATTLERS
WWW.AZRATTLERS.COM - @COACHKGUY

I started playing when I was five years old. My dad played football, my older brother played football. I had a brother that played linebacker at UAB. We had an athletic family. I went to the same high school as Bo Jackson. Being ten years younger than Bo, he was an idol to all of us. I was a big fan of his growing up. I was able to follow some of his successes. Our pee-wee program and pop warner group were really successful as a team, pretty much winning the championship every year.

When I was growing up, I was always little better than the kids at my age. I kind of knew that I had a shot to go on and play college football. I told myself at a young age that I was going to play football professionally. I never doubted that. I was 12 or 13 when I realized that I wanted to get into coaching when I was done playing. The coaches that I played for all had influences on me about life and football. No one in my family had ever coached before. I was told that I would be a good coach one day. That stuck with me. All of the coaches that I played for made me love coaching.

What I love most about the game of football? One is the strategy. It's not like any other sport. There's a lot of strategy that goes into the game. We always talk about situational football. How are we going to play the last minute of the half or the last minute of the game. It's very important. I enjoy the recruiting part of it as well. The Arena League gives you a little bit of what you get from the NFL and from college. In Arena Football, you have to coach your players but you also have to recruit them. It helped me to develop people skills and communicate better with people.

The other thing that I love about football is that you get to impose your will on other people on the field. One of the things that I always said; "I want to dominate my matchup." There are a lot of little things in football that require more than just coaching. I've been a mentor. I've been a temp service (laughs) trying to help guys find jobs in the off-season. There is a little bit of everything that goes into it. You develop a lot of skills. As a player, I loved dominating my matchup and imposing my will on my opponent. As a coach, I love the strategy. The challenge drew me to the game. Getting to go out there and compete. As a coach now the challenge is can you build a team? Can you put something together to compete and win a championship? Communication and trust are two things that you have to have to be successful.

I'd hope my football epitaph would say, "he came, he saw, he conquered." Another one would be "We will take non-believers and make them believers." This game teaches you so much about life and there are so many different things involved in it. The skills that you develop are skills that you can use in life.

ED REED

RETIRED NFL PLAYER

WWW.EDREEDFOUNDATION.ORG - @EDREED501C3

What I love about the game is that it brings people together. It brings a team together. It brings fans together. You could be going through the worst things in life and sports will bring kids together. When I was a kid, I stayed at the park watching my dad play basketball and football. Sports brought us together as a family. That's what football does. I love the fact that it does that. It brings people together from all walks of life. I met so many people because of football.

STEVE SMITH SR.
NFL WIDE RECEIVER - BALTIMORE RAVENS
@89SteveSmith

Players love the game for different reasons. Some play because of a desire to get out of their situations. Other people dream as a kid to play ball. I wanted to play ball because I dreamed of being in the 1,000 yard club. I remember having the 1,000 yard club football card of Carl Pickens. That's why I wanted to play. I just wanted to play ball.

Honestly, I play with passion because I have a fear of failure. I have a fear of not being good enough. That's what drives me to play hard and practice hard. I love to get my reps in practice. If I practice hard, I play hard. All of those things are constantly on my mind. I also love going out and winning a man-to-man match up and making my opponent look bad in front of his friends in the stands.

TERRY BOWDEN
HEAD COACH - UNIVERSITY OF AKRON
WWW.GOZIPS.COM - @TERRYBOWDEN

The biggest thing, just like my brother Tommy and I, our father has been a coach since 1955. We grew up as the sons of football coaches. When we reached 14, 15 years old, our dad was the head coach at West Virginia University. We saw him do it and wanted to do it too. It's like being in the family business. Our family business was coaching football. Our father was a good example. He made a good impression on us. It seemed like a great profession, we loved it. I gradually grew up in a household where college football was the family business. That's what got us there as far as the original interest that came in. That was the driving force. My dad has always been a great role model for the profession.

I wish I could tell you that one night I had an epiphany to become a head coach. I've always felt since middle school, junior high school that I wanted to get into it. At that point, you begin to picture being a head coach. We weren't star football players to become players at universities. You have to love to win. If you are going to sustain coaching for a long time, you have to love the arena. You have to love the competition, love competing, going out and being better than someone else. It's evaluated week to week. It never left us. When you're father is a role model and your mentor and he's extremely successful, you're home every day with him and you see the positive. You see the impact. You see your ability to impact younger people. That becomes an added value. Any great coach doesn't truly go into the profession to impact young people, you can be a boy scout leader or volunteer time to do that. Most coaches go in because they love playing football, competing and winning. If you see some purpose to your life, you see the value of helping young people and helping them grow.

The excitement, any coach that works the sideline loves the adrenaline, the excitement. I don't think there's anything like the excitement of being in the tunnel whether it's in Auburn going against Alabama or Akron going against Kent State. Standing in that tunnel waiting to go out in a big game, hearing the big crowd and the band playing the school song is exciting.

On the sideline, things happen in front of you and you have to react and move forward. It's the adrenaline of anyone that has played the game and knows the excitement. I've been fortunate enough to be a head coach in Division III, Division II and Division I. It doesn't need to be 100,000 out there, it does add to the excitement, but it doesn't change that much. There is an added adrenaline flow though. Going to Alabama, they're undefeated, you're undefeated or going against Penn State, Michigan in Ann Arbor, there's an added adrenaline.

I spent ten years in broadcasting. When I was in New York in NBC studios with John Saunders, it was live television. People ask why I like that. It's because it has the same adrenaline as being in the tunnel. You're waiting for the cameras to kick on knowing that you're live and anything that you do can't be repeated. You can't take it back. Football is a very stressful occupation but we would be lying if we did 't say that we love the adrenaline flow on game day.

Maybe I was the second best in the Bowden family. That would be a slap in my brother Tommy's face. (laughs) The bottom line would be at that at this point I've made an impact in young men's lives. The first quarterback that I signed out of high school was Jimbo Fisher. I have others but he was with me 14 years. Now I'm coaching the sons of players that I have coached. I've been doing that with many of the players that I've coached. I have made a difference in the player's lives. You want to make a difference in the community and the school. You want to look back and say that you have helped make a difference in player's lives.

JIM CATANZARO
HEAD COACH - LAKE FOREST COLLEGE
WWW.GOFORESTERS.COM - @LFC_FOOTBALL

Football is what we did in the neighborhood. The fun we were having playing in the front lawns or playing in the backyards, wherever it was, is what we did as kids. I remember we would go to the local school and tear up their front lawns because we weren't allowed on the field. So instead of hopping the fence, we just went on the front lawn of the school and tore that up instead; and we'd have everyone in the neighborhood do it. I remember we'd get our guys from the local park and then go over to another park and play those guys on a Sunday in a no pads, tackle football game. By the time we all got to junior high, we started the transition to organized football. That's when things really took off for me because I liked having a coach mentoring me through the process and teach me things. And there were a couple of coaches that were very influential to me. You want to talk about the power of influence; it was huge in my life. They saw something in me that had a chance to be really strong and really special. And I was able to run with that because what they allowed me to do and where they pointed me. They didn't hold my hand. They basically said, 'here's what you need to do, now go do it.' That was great, I really embraced that and it was enjoyable for me.

After college, I realized that I wanted football to be my career. We had a really unique situation at the college I went to. We had 40 incoming freshmen and only 3 seniors by the time of my senior year. So we had a lot of guys come and go. But the three guys that went through that process had something unique and special to fall upon. I actually thought I was going to go and become a high school teacher. I did my student teaching and hated it. I was miserable. So what I ended up doing was going to get a graduate degree, and I was fortunate enough to have a college coach say 'hey, you can get that paid for by being a graduate assistant at a small college.' He sent my information to a couple of people and I was able to get hired. Once I got into college coaching, I knew that's where I was supposed to be. The process of recruiting was appealing to me, which is something that a lot of guys don't like. I enjoyed it! I like meeting new people and sitting in living rooms explaining why our university had an advantage. In this situation, my focus has sort of shifted because I've seen guys go from freshman year to graduation. And there's something unique and special when you go to that graduation, and you see those guys, many of whom are 1st generation college students, walk across that stage and get their degree, but in the other hand is a conference championship ring. And the pride that they have in that with each other is something that's really unique and special. They know what it took to get there because they are not easy to come by.

I was lucky, my third year in coaching we won a conference championship. I got hooked right at that moment and I wanted our guys, whomever we were coaching, to have that experience.

The emotional release is what I truly love about the game of football. Whether it's an exciting play that gets you all jacked up and juiced, or it's the fact that you're able to pour everything that you have into a play. Whatever frustration you had that week, you can put it into that first kickoff coverage, that first block you may have or whatever it might be, you get the chance to release a lot of emotion that you otherwise, have no place to release. There's nothing else like that. My wife's a runner and she gets that high from running. That does nothing for me. I want to go out there and get rid of something physically and it's something that you can pour yourself into. And when you come off the field, even as a coach, you know you've given it your all and you left something out there. And the players get that too. There's something about the total commitment, that 'leaving it all on the field' component that's really special and unique.

I want there to be a bunch of players, when they come to see me, the last thing they talk about is wins and losses. I want them to come and talk to me about a story or something that I may have done for them that had nothing to do with us winning or losing a game. I hope they have something that they took with them far past their playing days; a life lesson or whatever it might be. I want there to be something that I helped add to their world that had nothing to do with football. Whether it's the way they approach or handle things, whatever it is, that's what I want them to talk about. I don't care what my record is at the end of my career, and the wins and losses for games, I only care about the wins and losses with the players and the impact we were able to have on them, to help make them better people.

DINO BABERS

Head Coach - Bowling Green State University
www.bgsufalcons.com - @CoachBabersBG

I was a short fat kid and I was a 'momma's boy'. My dad played football, my older brother played football and my younger brother played football and all I wanted to do was stay in the house and eat. My older brother used to basically beat me up and make me go outside and play football. That's how I started playing, so I wouldn't get beat up.

I always knew I wanted to be a football coach but never knew I wanted to be a football player. When I was younger, I always wanted to watch football on television and that was my brother's issue with me. My brother would always say, 'You watch it why don't you go play it?' I didn't want to play; I just wanted to coach it.

By watching football, it made me start to really love the game. Then I wanted to learn the nuances of the game; that got me better. That got me good enough to play in high school, get a scholarship and have an opportunity to play in Canada before I got let go. But my love for the game always came from the coaching aspect; I just learned to become a good player. The coolest thing about football is that it's the closest thing to being fair in the world to me. That's even with the referees making mistakes. It's one guy against another guy regardless of size, weight, background, color, creed and you've got an opportunity to have success minus the political ramifications that go on in the world. "

I want to win, but I want to win the right way. I want to win in the right way not only on the football field with my players but after my players leave me, I want them to be better fathers, better sons and better husbands. I think if you can win on the field the right way, not cheating, not cutting corners, doing it the way it needs to be done playing by the rules, you give these young men an opportunity after their finished playing to make them a part of a tradition. Making those guys a part of a legacy, or part of something they can be proud of so that they go on to be fathers, husbands and sons and teach their kids that kind of pride, character is what's important to me. That's something I'd like to see on my football tombstone.

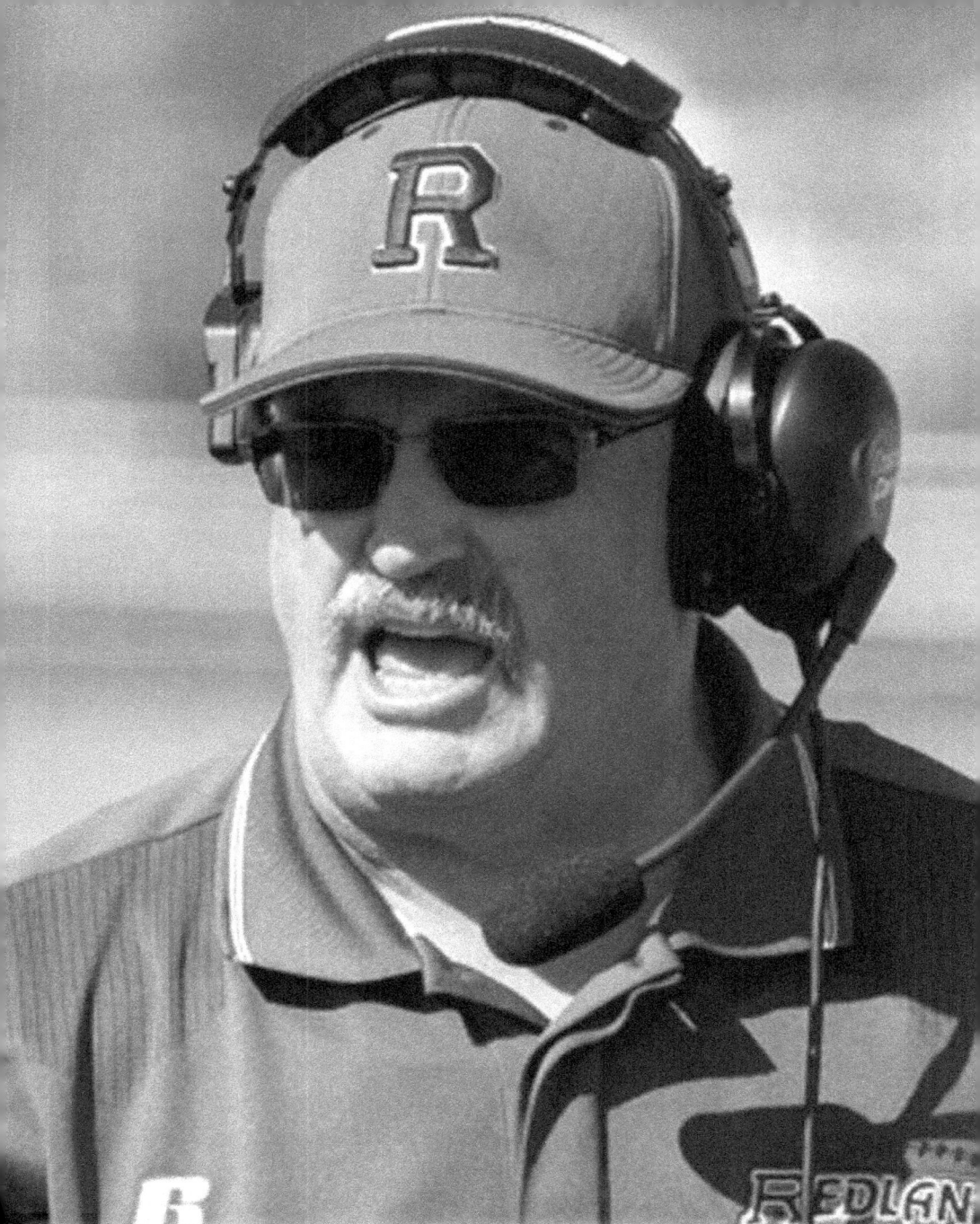

MIKE MAYNARD

HEAD COACH - UNIVERSITY OF THE REDLANDS

WWW.REDLANDS.EDU - @UofR_FOOTBALL

I grew up the son of a high school coach in Illinois. I grew up around football, jumping over bags, chasing balls, scraping the mud off of cleats; basically doing whatever I could because I loved being a part of that whole environment. I loved hanging out with my dad. Since he was always coaching, there wasn't really any other way to have time with him other than going to practice everyday and be a part of his experience with his high school team. In the Midwest where I grew up, there's not much to do. So football was an avenue for us to have fun. It was always a game that was fun to play, and I enjoyed that experience.

It was some time when I was 4 or 5 years old. The neighborhood kids that were older than me said I couldn't play in the game. They were playing in someone's backyard and they said I couldn't play because I wasn't old enough. I remember running home and getting my dad's whistle, coaching hat and running back to the backyard and saying 'well if I can't play, then I'll be the coach'. I remember that experience. And I remember doing that more than a couple of times, being the coach for the older guys because they thought that I was too young to play. So in a way, I always knew that my best thing would end up being coaching.

As a coach, I always enjoyed the schematic part of football. I always enjoyed understanding the scheme, the game plan, the X's and O's part of the game; I loved the how you could get an advantage over an opponent by scheming, whether it was offense, defense or special teams. I always wanted to figure that out. From a player standpoint, I always enjoyed the rugged, toughness and the training for the sport. I always like to be around those that were training with me. I felt a real kinship and fellowship with those that loved being on a team. I think the teamwork involved, the scheme and strategy part of it, was a big part of my enjoyment of the game. I just loved the whole preparation part of the experience. I love the preparing in the offseason and getting ready for the following season. Lastly, I loved the success part of the game. Working hard and proving ourselves successful as a team, made me feel really satisfied. A group of guys working hard, seeing that goal realized, and become successful just made it a real joyful experience.

As a coach, I want to be remembered as a person who knew how to win, and who knew how to teach others to win. I want to be remembered as a person that always had the right attitude, who had impeccable character, and as a person that always worked hard toward a goal. I think that would summarize what I ultimately would like to be remembered for as a coach.

JD HARRIS

OWNER - HI-INTENSITY SPORTS CONCEPT

FORMER NFL SCOUT & COLLEGE FOOTBALL COACH
WWW.HI-INTENSITYSPORTS.COM - @COACHJDHARRIS

For as long as I could remember, I was taken by the game of football. I always remember just having a football. Growing up in Chicago, watching the Bears when they had Walter Payton and Roland Harper, who was a family friend, it was just something I had to do. It was something that was in me and I started playing when I was 4 years old.

When I was out there playing ball in junior high school, we had so many good athletes that played multiple sports and I'm a visionary; I knew that one day, I was going to play college football. Now my size didn't always determine that; as a matter of fact, it said the opposite. The more doubt that came my way because of my size, was just more motivation I was given to pursue my goals of playing football and ultimately coaching it. The first 'high' I got playing football was when I ran the option. I was a quarterback and it just felt like time froze. It was such a unique feeling that I can't even begin to explain. Now, I've never done drugs or anything like that, but I can imagine that this is what getting high must feel like and that's what football became for me.

I love that football is unpredictable. It takes a brotherhood to band together, a lot of people from diverse backgrounds, to come together and move on one accord. It's that camaraderie that's very hard to replace. The strategy involved is something that I love about the game as well. It's not just your body that's put to the test, but your mind and your will to succeed are tested also. So there are all of these different components that make football very intriguing. It's like the game of chess with live people. I would hope my legacy would be that I was a fierce competitor, who loved to develop people, and who had a desire to win. I want to use the game of football as a conduit to change the world because the influence that's attached to it.

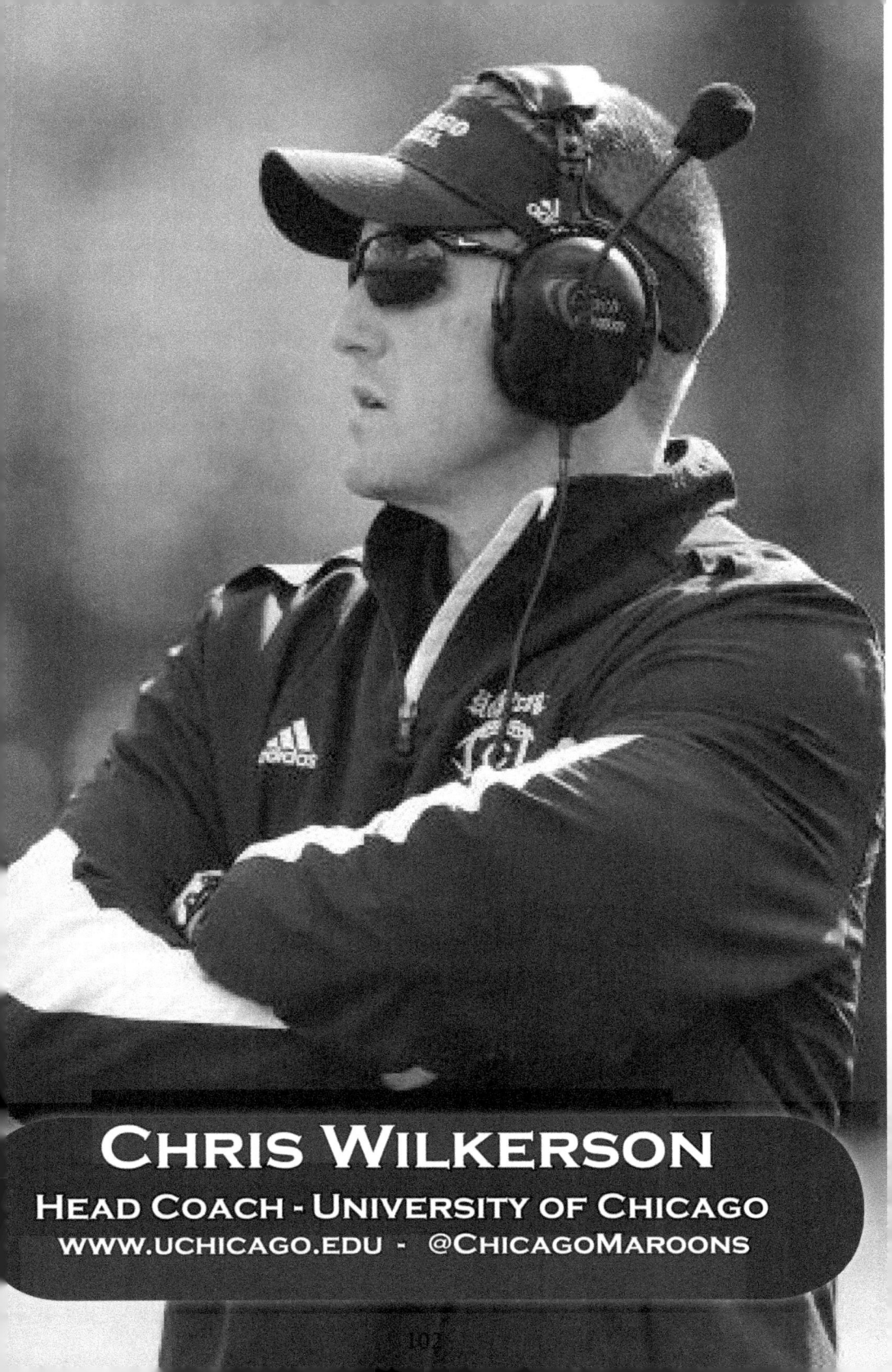

CHRIS WILKERSON
HEAD COACH - UNIVERSITY OF CHICAGO
WWW.UCHICAGO.EDU - @CHICAGOMAROONS

I got a later start than a lot of people. I didn't start playing football until the 7th grade. I think at the beginning, to be completely honest with you, I think that my mom thought 'boy this is going to be practice 5 nights a week and I'm not going to have to worry about him after school.' But I just fell in love with it as a player during that 7th grade season. I was very fortunate that I got to play in junior high and into high school, which ultimately lead to me earning a football scholarship to Eastern Illinois University.

But the biggest reason that I got into coaching is because of the impact that coaches had on me as a young person. My mom and dad divorced when I was extremely young and the men that were around me a ton, were very influential to me, and my continued development as a young man were coaches. I valued the lessons that I learned and the relationships that I built competing in football. So when I got done and had the opportunity to stay and coach at the college level, I took it. It's just an amazing experience. It's the ability to impact others and help people be the best that they can be. I love being a mentor and helping kids reach their potential. It's just an amazing game! I know they say that coaches have a tendency to reach more people maybe in one year, than many will do in a lifetime. And I value that opportunity to reach young people.

When I went to college, I knew that I wanted to teach and coach. I was hoping to coach football and probably track and field, but I always thought that it would be at the high school level. But I had such a great experience in college with my position coach Randy Melvin, who's now the defensive line coach at the University of Miami, my head coach Bob Spoo kind of became a second father to me, so it was just an amazing experience with all of the guys that I was around. Coach asked me after I was done, and I was doing my student teaching, if I thought about coaching college football? I hadn't thought about it and he said that he thought I'd be pretty good and wanted me to come help out in the spring. So I did, I fell in love with it and haven't done anything else since. I feel blessed that I haven't done anything else other than being a college football coach since I graduated from Eastern Illinois University. It's been a lot of fun!

I think it's the ability to compete is what I love the most about the game. Whether it's competing on game day or in your preparation leading up to it, or even just competing versus other schools, not just on the field, but in the recruiting process, and that's for both players and coaches, that competition is a rush. I really like everything that goes into it; the preparation, the camaraderie and the relationships that you build.

I still keep in great contact with guys that I coached with back in 1995. The new General Manager for the Chicago Bears, Ryan Pace, was a freshman defensive end for me at Eastern Illinois University. To coach Ryan all five years, and was a team captain for us as well, I knew he wanted to get into the NFL. He wanted it so bad that he jumped into his beat up car, drove all the way down to New Orleans, and sat around all day with no guarantee that he'd get in front of somebody, just to interview for an unpaid internship. He was very fortunate that he got his foot in the door and worked his tail off doing a great job with Sean Payton. Now he has this tremendous opportunity to be the General Manager of the Chicago Bears. That to me is what it's all about.

To me, it's so much more than about the wins and the losses. Now they do keep score and I'm as competitive as anybody, but I hope that when it's all said and done, and people want to talk about me as a football coach or as a person, I hope that they say that I was a good person and helped them become an even better person. I want them to be able to say that Coach Wilkerson help prepare me for life after college. I hope that when guys leave these walls at the University of Chicago, that if they have to deal with any type of adversity, they feel as though they're more prepared based on their time spent with me. We try to have a great time while we're here, it's not always easy love and there's some tough love that's involved, but it is very important to me that they leave here as prepared as they possibly can for the remainder of their life.

CARL BANKS

FORMER NFL LINEBACKER, ENTREPRENEUR

G-III SPORTS BY CARL BANKS - @CARLBANKSGIII

Curiosity initially drew me into the game of football. I moved to a new neighborhood and I saw these kids playing pop warner. I was 8 years old and I saw that the kids had full equipment on. I went down to ask the coach how much does it cost to play football? He said that it doesn't cost anything; you just need your parents' permission. So, I went home and got my parents' permission and joined the team. That's what initially got me into football and just the whole 'being a part of a team' aspect of it

I never really had the luxury of 'scripting' my career the way that many do or have done. Every team I was on, I was probably the 4th or 5th best player on the team. And that was elementary through high school. I thought I was going to be a basketball player actually. I was a pretty good high school basketball player and a three-sport athlete; they made us play everything. So, I thought basketball would be my thing but it ended up being football. I didn't know how good I would be. I was a good athlete, but I played offensive line and defensive line in high school because I was one of the biggest guys on the team.

I was getting recruited by all of the Big Ten schools and schools like Oklahoma and a few other big schools. I ended up going to Michigan State, they were just coming off of probation, and they were hurting for scholarships and everything. I had a lot of opportunities to go elsewhere but Magic Johnson, whom I met a basketball camp, told me that I would love Michigan State and wouldn't regret it; and I didn't. But that being said, we weren't very good in the Big Ten as a whole. I did make 1st Team All-Big Ten for three straight years. So I knew I had some talent, but then I was looking in these college football magazines at the time and see some of the really big names like Wilber Marshall, Ricky Huntley, Jackie Shipp, all these different guys and I'm thinking, man these guys must be really good! When my senior season was over with, I didn't get invited to any of the all-star games or NFL combine. My head coach at the time George Perles thought I was good enough and he said that he could get me into a game that no one wants to play in but all of the NFL Scouts and coaches are there. It was the Blue-Gray Game down in Montgomery, Alabama. It was cold and played on Christmas Day, but I got the chance to showcase my skills in front of all of the NFL coaches. So by the time I got home from that game, in which I was the MVP, I got invited to the NFL combine, the Senior Bowl and a couple of other games. So it worked out pretty well for me.

But just understanding that I didn't have the luxury of really knowing or scripting my path to where I would go was interesting. And then to get drafted by the New York Giants, who had 4 All-Pro linebackers, I was like 'here we go again' (laughs), but it worked out okay. For me, making sure I had something outside of college was important. I was able to get my degree and focus on the communication skills that I was looking to acquire. I thought I wanted to write commercials for a living when I was in college because I had so much fun.

The competitiveness is what I truly love the most about the game. When you have the opportunity to succeed or fail and in 45 seconds, you get up and do it again? It's the ultimate game! Football is a game of instantaneous results. And that component is what I love most about the game, on the field. Off the field, it was the training and the setting of goals that I loved. That is something that really drove me every offseason. The whole working on something that I wasn't good at was a challenge that I enjoyed accepting. I always looked at who the best was and tried to be better or at least as good. Then applying that in training camp. I swear, it's the competitiveness that really drove me as a player. I would hope that people remember me as a guy that played the game hard, competitively and that I was hell of a technician.

BRANDON HOWARD

MIAMI DOLPHINS INSIDER - SPORTS TALK FLORIDA
WWW.SPORTSTALKFLORIDA.COM - @DASHDIALLO1

Growing up in Columbus, Ohio as a Cleveland Browns' fan, my life was changed forever when the Browns selected Eric Metcalf in the 1989 NFL Draft. From the moment I saw him take a handoff, I knew I wanted to be just like him. I also participated in sprints and the long jump in the Junior Olympics and aimed for all of Metcalf's youth records. I was glued to the television every Sunday because of Metcalf.

After graduating from college I took a seven-year break from football. I wouldn't watch it on television and frankly didn't want to speak about it. Slowly but surely, with the advent of Twitter I found myself wanting to share my knowledge of the game with others. I was given an opportunity to write about the game I love. At that point, I realized that I never wanted to leave the game again.

The friendships that are formed through football are like no other. The work you put in with your teammates creates that bond. No one understands what you go through just to play a game, but you and your contemporaries. The friends that you make through football last a lifetime. He took the time to learn all he could from the game from a mental and physical perspective. I'd also like to be remembered as someone who took the time to give back to the youth.

JOE MOORHEAD
HEAD COACH - FORDHAM UNIVERSITY
WWW.FORDHAMSPORTS.COM - @BALLCOACHJOEMO

Well…if you grow up in the western Pennsylvania area in Pittsburgh, I don't want to say it's a birthright but if you're a kid that's athletic and competitive, you're drawn to the game of football. Whether it's rooting for the Pittsburgh Steelers or the University of Pittsburgh, it's sort of in you. My dad coached our Catholic school team, my older brother played, so it's just something you grow up in. You're outside playing pickup football and the first opportunity you get to play in a tackle league, you get in it. So I don't think I ever made a conscious decision to play football, I just think it's something in the water back home.

I really look back to my days playing grade school football at some of the coaches I played for in 5th-8th grade as some of the greatest guys who taught me what the game was about and kind of stoked my competitive spirit. I always talk about the consequence of preparation and execution. It wasn't a situation where you're in 5th grade and everyone gets a participation medal and telling you that everything is all good, these coaches drove us to be our best. I think at that young age with coaches who were that influential in caring about developing you as a football player, was vital. Two of the things that are great about football: the accountability and the discipline. That really set the path going into high school, into my playing days at Fordham and a little bit after in the Arena League. When your identity is forged in the sport, and like I said, you're indebted to all of the great things that football has done for you academically, athletically and then the camaraderie part of it as well, it's tough to lose that. When I was cut from the Arena League and I had that long drive home from Milwaukee to Pittsburgh, part of your identity is pulled from you. And I couldn't think of anything better to do to fill that void that you had as a football player than to get into coaching.

You get chills just thinking about it. First and foremost, I think it's the competitive aspect of the game that I love the most. You work 365 days a year for only 10-12 opportunities per season, with a chance to play a few more. It's not just the Friday night lights, the Saturday afternoons or Sundays that people see; it's all of the other things that go into that. It's the 6am workouts; the summer running and conditioning when everyone else is in the pool or at the playground. So it's the combination of the competitive aspect where you get to go out as a team, which I think is the most unique team sport in the world, you're dependent on the performance of 11 other people to have success, as opposed maybe some other sports.

The preparation and camaraderie is where friendships are forged with people whom you may never meet in another walk of life. But when you get in-between those white lines and in the locker room, it doesn't matter where you're from, how much money you make, what race you are, you're only talking about a certain amount of people that are united for a common goal. There's nothing sweeter than a group of guys and coaching staff doing all of the things necessary to prepare for a game and going out there an executing it. That's really what it's all about.

I would want my football tombstone to read, that I was a great Christian, great father, and a great coach in that order. I would want it to be known that as a player and a coach, I treated the game with respect, gave it everything I had and as a player I was fortunate enough to be able to go to college and have an opportunity to play off of that because of this great game. As a coach, having the opportunity to impact the lives of your position players, the guys you recruit and the kids on the team in a positive manner to help them achieve their potential academically, athletically and socially. Ultimately, we as coaches are educators. It's not just about the wins or the team/individual accolades. Part of the beauty of this profession is seeing a kid walk across the stage and get his college degree while using football as a vehicle to set that up. We have guys that go on and play at the next level and that's great. We tell our guys that it's great if the NFL is your goal as long as it isn't your only goal. But for me, I'm just as proud of the guys that have the opportunity to go on to the NFL, whether it was here or at UConn with guys like Marcus Easley, Jordan Todman and all of those guys; or at Akron with Domenik Hixson. I'm just as proud of those guys as I am of the guys that leave here with their degrees, and go on to great successes both professionally, and personally. I think it's great to be in a position to be able to set guys up for success in the future.

DARON FRANKLIN

SAFETIES COACH/SPECIAL TEAMS COORDINATOR

JOHN EHRET HIGH SCHOOL (LA)

@COACH_DFRANK

I can remember just watching football with my dad at home and being around my older cousins who were playing football at the time, that's initially what drew me in. So, at about 7 or 8 years old, that's when I started playing at Milne Playground in New Orleans. Just seeing the excitement, the passion, the teamwork and the camaraderie on TV is what made me really fall in love with the game. At that time, as a young kid, Jerry Rice was my favorite player; and guy like Ronnie Lott, was my favorite defensive player because of his physical toughness. The game just looked so exciting on TV that I had to go and play it.

During college I had an experience that sort of put me on this current path. I did my internship in New Orleans and I came home from Langston University. And I had the chance to workout with some NFL guys at Tom Shaw's facility. I saw that during the workout, even though I was from a small school, I was able to compete and hold my own against these guys that I saw on TV. That motivated me to continue to chase the dream of playing professionally. I went back to Langston University and had a pretty good senior season before it was cut short due to injury. But after that, I was able to play a couple of years of professional ball against guys that I saw on TV in college as well as some guys that played in the NFL. I quickly found out that it was more about opportunity and if you applied yourself, you could continue to chase your dreams and move up to a high level.

Now that I'm on the coaching side, it's the gratitude you get from being able to build young men. When they come back to visit and say 'hey coach, thanks for showing me how to do x-y-z,' whether it's on the field or off of it. It's those experiences that you love the most. At the time I was able to actually hire one of my former players to join the staff and coach with me. Which was humbling because of all the places he could've gone, he wanted to come and coach with me. That sort of lets me know that I'm at least doing things the right way. It's always bigger than football with me.

For me, whatever my impact on the game was or will be, it will always deal with education. My players, current and former, would be able to tell you the same thing. I always say that, football is a vehicle but education is the driver to get you where you need to go.

If you were to ask any of my players, they'll say 'Coach Franklin help me in school; helped me communicate with teachers and build relationships with people; he was always a stickler for making sure I applied myself in the classroom, so if I didn't have an opportunity to play football beyond high school, I could at least be a productive citizen in society.' So, a large part of my legacy would be about education and probably the second part would be about the energy and intensity I brought to the game of football. I really just enjoy being able to teach the game of football to the next generation.

JEFF TEDFORD
HEAD COACH - B.C. LIONS
WWW.BCLIONS.COM - @COACHTEDFORD

My brother was the biggest influence as a youngster. He played football and was kind of my father figure. He encouraged me to play the game, put me around it and spent time with me. I started playing when I was 8-years old, but my brother was really the person that jumpstarted my interest in the sport.

There was a really defining moment in my life in regards to football. I was a freshman in high school. I was coming from a single-parent home; wasn't a big guy, a late-developer for sure. I was wondering around outside of the varsity coach's office. Just sort of wondering, not knowing what to do with myself after school one day. Coach took the time to call me up to his office; we sat down and talked for a little bit over an hour mostly about what I wanted to do and things of that nature. Now, I'm a little, skinny freshman kid and he's the varsity coach; now he has no idea that I'll turn out to be a pretty good football player but he took the time with me, and at that time right then, it was the motivation and having him taking an interest in me was something that really pushed me over the top, not just to play football, but for it to ultimately become what I wanted to do for a living. So, me choosing football for a career path really started in high school. He was the first coach that really made a difference in my life. He left after my freshman year, and the coaches who took over, just continued that positive reinforcement. It was my mentors in high school and then when I went on to play Junior College for that same coach, who was the varsity coach my freshman year in high school. So, I was just fortunate every step of the way to have great mentors that were coaches. They really made a big difference in my life, and motivated me to go in the right direction. All of that, led to my decision to want to follow in their footsteps.

The camaraderie and the competition are the two things I love about the game. When people talk about 'life after football,' they have a hard time understanding why people have a hard time with that. When you play football for so long, it's really the built-in support system for friendship and camaraderie that you don't find everywhere. It's not about the accolades, or all those things, but camaraderie that you get in the locker room everyday, the structure that's been provided for you your whole life, all of a sudden you don't have that structure, it's a huge change. So, I loved the structure and the camaraderie that came along with the game, both as a player and a coach. I hope people would look back and say that I was a good teammate, and as far as a coach, helped guide young people toward a path of growth and development in all areas, not just football.

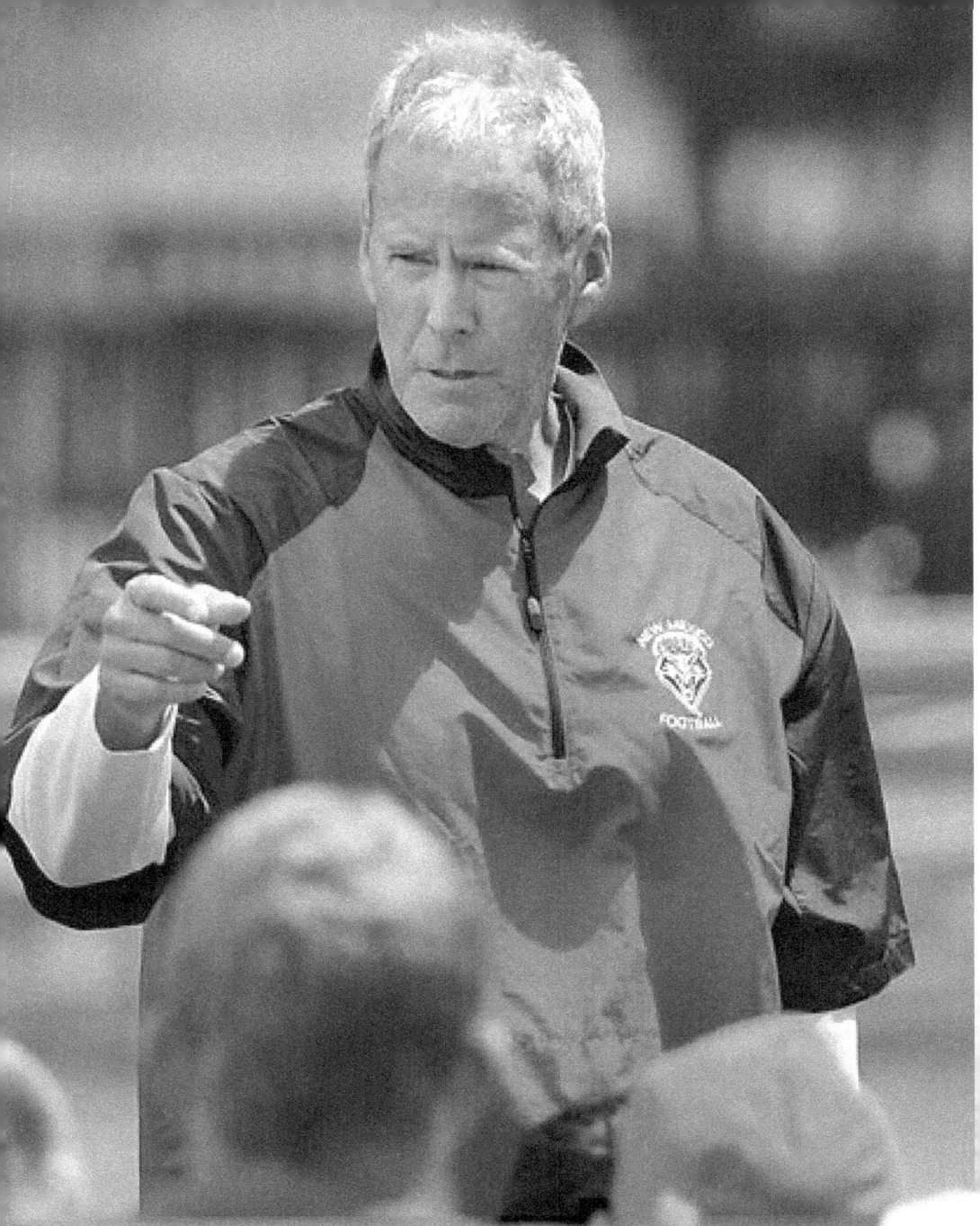

BOB DAVIE
HEAD COACH - UNIVERSITY OF NEW MEXICO
WWW.GOLOBOS.COM - @UNMLOBOS

Obviously I grew up in Pittsburgh and sports were a major part of my life from as long as I could remember. But from the football standpoint, what got me into it was as a young guy, everyone in my community went to the high school football games on Friday night. Just Friday night football games and standing outside that fence when the players came into the stadium, or when the players left the stadium after the game, and you'd be hollering for the mouthpiece or for a sweatband, and I just held those guys in such high regards. I played all sports but I think football directly was a result of going to high school games on Friday nights and then seeing the high school players wear their jerseys on Friday in school at high school, it was such a big deal. I grew up in an area of the country where football was held in such high regard and still is, so I think I played all sports but it kind of goes back to the Friday night football under the lights and how big that was in the community I lived in.

I knew early on that sports would be some part of my life. Obviously growing up, you don't know what the opportunities are going to be or how you can make a living out of doing it. There was probably the first phase where you thought you were going to be good enough as a player but that quickly went out the window. When I was in college, I knew I was going to teach and coach but at that time it was the high school Phys Ed teacher thing and go back to coach high school football. My senior year in college at Youngstown State University, a new coaching staff came in and there was a young assistant coach that had taken over as the offensive coordinator. He came in for his first year and we were about three or four games into the season, we were really struggling and we had a lot of success the year before but our offense wasn't doing very well. He came by my dormitory on a Monday or Tuesday night during the season and said 'man, can I just talk to you? I just want to talk about the team and what guys are saying and do you have any opinion on this because you've been here for a while.' And we sat and talked for an hour or so, and at the end of the conversation, he said have you ever thought about going into coaching? I said yeah. I'm thinking about hopefully graduating and going on to be a phys ed teacher and coaching high school. He said 'no, I'm talking about college coaching.' Have you ever thought about becoming a graduate assistant and going the college route? I didn't even know you can do that or that was even possible. A light went off, and I went on to become a graduate assistant coach at the University of Pittsburgh right out of college.

And it went back to that conversation with that assistant football coach that came by my room mentioning at the end of the conversation 'have you thought about coaching' and directing me into college coaching by becoming a graduate assistant. So that's how the whole thing happened.

It's camaraderie, the competition, just the day in and day out being surrounded by people that really care that keeps me in the game. Football to me is the greatest game of all. All sports are great, but football is hard and football eliminates the pretenders. It's the camaraderie and the competition at the end of the day and I truly believe this game really does build character. In this game, true character comes out because there is nowhere to hide and that's what I love about it. There's no place for the pretender in this and the pretenders get exposed.

I hope looking back, people would say that I was fairly successful in my coaching career, but was even more successful in my personal life and was able to keep the balance with his family. So, I was able to be somewhat successful in the coaching profession but never at the cost of my family. I'd hope they'd say that 'he might have been a good coach, but was a great father and a great husband.'

JERRY MACK

HEAD COACH - NORTH CAROLINA CENTRAL UNIVERSITY
WWW.NCCUEAGLEPRIDE.COM - @NCCU_FOOTBALL

Growing up, the thing that drove me to the game of football was that it's such a competitive sport, it's the ultimate team sport. I wasn't always the strongest and fastest but I could still find a way to nurture my craft and be good at certain things. I developed a love for the game by watching the game. My dad was a football player; he was the first walk-on captain at the level that he had played.

I developed a passion for the teaching of the game in high school. I really enjoyed being coach; I enjoyed coaches and felt that they played a deep part in development. I had a great respect for coaches. What really changed it all was when I was going into my senior year in college. I got a chance to go on a recruiting visit with my position coach. I saw how he communicated with potential recruits. We went to high schools and when we got back, he told me that I would be a great coach. When he said that, I really thought about how I could do something that I allowed me to be around the game that I love. I really thought about giving coaching a try. That car ride with my position coach really got me thinking about it.

I love the strategic part of it. I love being able to match wits with the offense and defense, figuring out what the best scheme would be and how to put players in the best situation to be successful. If you're willing to learn and work hard, coaches will put you in position to be successful. Football is 50% talent, the rest of it is about how hard you work, how smart you are on and off the field as far as making decisions.

Hard work beats talent when talent doesn't work hard.

BRET BIELEMA

HEAD COACH - UNIVERSITY OF ARKANSAS

WWW.RAZORBACKFB.COM - @BRETBIELEMA

I idolized my older brothers Bart and Barry. My grandfather didn't let my father play because he came from a pretty strict Dutch background. My father never really pushed us to play football but he was always very excited when we were around it.

I didn't play organized football until 10th grade and I fell in love with it. I was a quarterback and a middle linebacker. I didn't know it at the time, but I was put in leadership roles from the beginning. I liked the ability to influence people around me. I had a lot of success. Through high school, I had a chance to go on and play in college. In college I never thought about coaching until my second or third year in college after being influenced by the staff that I was around. The competitive nature of winning and losing is what I love the most. I think that everyone can say that there are a lot of things that go into it but for me it's the competitive nature necessary to have success. It puts a lot on you but it's also very rewarding and it's something I really thrive off of.

I would hope everyone would say that I'm the same guy everyday. That's the one thing I try to be; I try to be as consistent as possible. He was the same coach everyday and win or lose he tried to make us better.

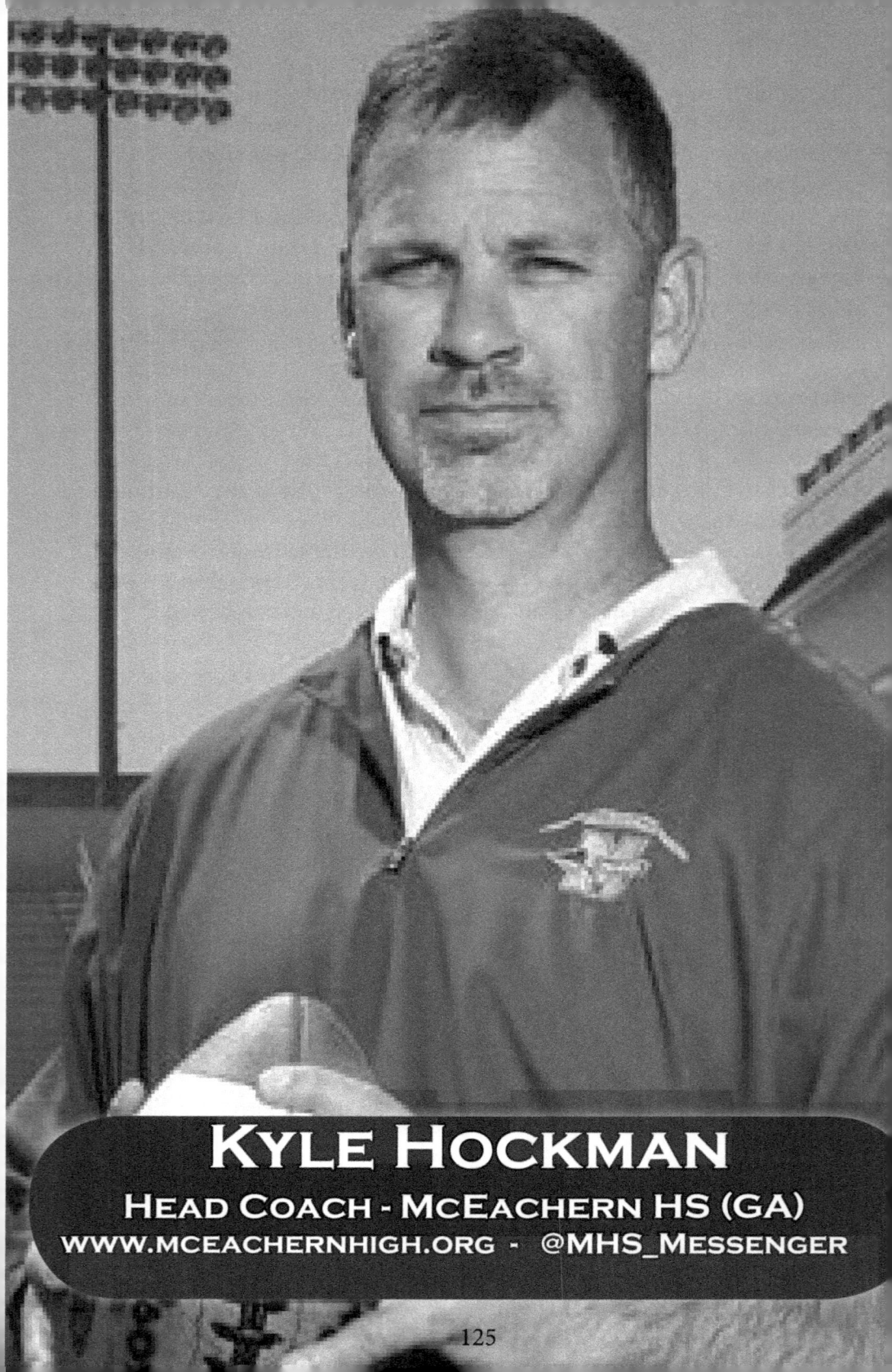

KYLE HOCKMAN
HEAD COACH - McEACHERN HS (GA)
WWW.MCEACHERNHIGH.ORG - @MHS_MESSENGER

Coming at it from the perspective of my old man, he was a really successful high school football coach; and I've been around it (the game) since I could remember. You know, hanging out, watching practice, being on the dummies, all of the practices, the two-a-days…all of that stuff, being a ball boy. The high school football players were my heroes. That whole small town high school football mentality, drawing the town together, the community and everybody 'wanting to be a Tiger', was something that we all grew up with. So, for me, that was the initial part of it and we had a lot of great family times around high school football.

I started playing when I was in 4th grade and had, you know, limited success. I was 'decent'. I wasn't the star of the team or anything along those lines. But it was the whole idea of playing peewee ball, wearing the same colors as the high school team and being able to wear your jersey to school on game day was more of community aspect or social part of it that really drew me in initially, more so than the actual 'love of the game' at that age.

I realized about the middle of my high school career, maybe my junior year I think it was, that naturally being around it for so long, that I sort of knew what was going on and translated into me instructing other players what to do. I wasn't the quarterback, the middle linebacker or the free safety. I was never playing any of those positions that made the calls, but I always seemed to have a good feel or understanding for what the opponents were doing and those kinds of things. And this went on into college when I was playing, picking up playbooks fairly easily and was kind of the 'student of the game'. I was a guy who was physically capable; a 3-year starter in both football and baseball at Bowling Green, becoming All-Conference in both sports my senior year, so I was fairly decent. I knew I wasn't an NFL player or even a Major League/Minor League Baseball player but I had enough success, especially with the cerebral or knowledge of the game part, the leadership and 'tough times' part more than my physical abilities. Now, having said all of that, and having it in my family and watching dad do it, was a big part of the whole process of getting into coaching. So, I knew from a pretty young age, maybe high school that this is what I was going to do. You know I had the dreams, the aspirations of doing the college thing, I thought I was going to be Bobby Bowden or one of those legends (laughter).

I remember in my early coaching career, I worked the Bowden Passing Academy. It involved the top quarterbacks and wide receivers in the southeast, and all of the Bowden boys. I got a chance to work with him. It was about 10 coaches, all good coaches, and besides the Bowdens, you know all of the other coaches very well. They were very prominent coaches…except my brother and I. I never thought to get an autograph or picture with the guy, because I'm thinking, 'I'm going to be Bobby Bowden one day' and this is nothing out of the ordinary. I mean, looking back on it… Jimbo Fisher, Rich Rodriguez, Terry, Tommy & Jeff (Bowden), I was working side-by-side with these guys at the camp, so I knew that I enjoyed coaching and that was the direction that I wanted to go.

Coming from the perspective of the 'cerebral' player and knowing the game, knowing the intricacies of how hard it is to get 11 guys to execute a play and be really good at it, I would say the strategic part of the game is what I love the most; both as a player and a coach. Especially early in my career, seeing the execution and the impact of technique, would really be gratifying as a coach to see it happing during the game and on film, and to think that I had a little something to do with the success of other people. That was the young coach in me, sort of taking credit for that, now my thoughts have evolved and it's more about the kids, enjoying the time, seeing them come back and tell you what you meant to them in helping them become young men. I love that aspect of coaching. If you help them have success on the field, then they'll listen to you and then, you can help them have success in life.

I like to think that through the game of football, teaching young kids all about life while having fun doing it would be something that I hope everyone remembers and understands.

BRIAN CRIST

WIDE RECEIVERS COACH - YOUNGSTOWN STATE UNIVERSITY
WWW.YSUSPORTS.COM - @COACHCRIST1

My dad was a football coach so he could tell you that ever since I was 6 years old, this is something I've always wanted to do. He was the coach at my high school for 40 years. But that's really what drew me into it; it was the fact that my dad did it. I think a lot of kids tend to do what their parents did especially when you're young and impressionable, and you see them have enjoyment in what they're doing, that makes you want to follow them. So if someone was to come home everyday miserable from their job, I don't think their kid would want to follow them. I always enjoyed the game of football, but when I got older, I always wanted to have an impact on people like my dad did as a coach.

As a 5'10 ½ quarterback, I knew my chances of playing professional were slim, so I had to figure out something else and my strength as a player, especially growing up with my dad being a coach, was the mental part of the game. So, I wanted to just keep doing that part of it. I felt that coaching was the only way where you could get that same feeling of competing that you got as a player. Once my playing career was done, coaching gave me that same feeling of competing against another, finding out how good you really were and being a part of a team environment.

Football is just a great game. And I don't think that I'd be even close to the same person I am today if it wasn't for football. Now I don't know how I would be different, but everything I've done, most of the decisions I make, how I treat people, the way I go about doing my job or raising my family it somehow relates back to when I was a player, or something my dad did as a coach, or something I did while coaching. I remember when I was out of D1 coaching for a season or two and I was coaching D3 ball and high school ball, I remember entertaining the thought of doing something else, every time I'd meet with a headhunter or recruiter they'd always ask 'well, what do you want to do?' and I'd say I don't know because all I want to do is coach. So, I couldn't see myself doing anything else. Would I be successful doing something else? Sure. But I don't want to do anything else. I mean football is a 365-day type deal. Even if you're not actually coaching or playing, you're constantly thinking about it. I don't know if there's any other career where you're constantly thinking about it all the time. Away from what people would call 'success' like winning championships and all of that, I would really hope that people would say that I got the most out of the players I coached and gave them an opportunity to be successful, not only on the field, but for the rest of their life. I learned from my dad that your job and duty as a coach is to make your players better; and that's better football players; better people; better students; better husbands and better fathers.

ANTHONY BECHT

ORMER NFL PLAYER, ESPN COLLEGE FOOTBALL ANALYST

TAMPA BAY BUCS ANALYST 620 WDAE AM

WWW.ANTHONYBECHTFOOTBALLCAMP.COM - @ANTHONY_BECHT

Growing up as a kid, the biggest thing for me was my diversity in sports. I played football, basketball, baseball, and ran track. Football was my least favorite as kid but for me, it was all about being around my friends and teammates, having fun. It was fun being a part of a team that was always in the mix to win.

My junior year of high school is when I started getting some love. We had a good football team. I was probably top 5 or 6 on my team. I was in the mix of a lot of good players. We pushed each other hard and won a championship. I wasn't a blue chip All-American going into college. I was a project going into college at West Virginia. I started seeing my name in those magazines during my junior year at West Virginia and I started to think that there was a shot to take it to the next level. That's really when I started to hone in.

I think for me, being a part of it was staying relevant. My only identity over the years was playing football. Football was my life. There was a time right after when I retired that I thought something would pop up. That structure in doing things, having something that makes you relevant in life is what kept me involved in the game. I remember doing a golf event and Carl Lewis was speaking to me. He asked me what I did and I told him that I play in the NFL. He asked me what I was going to do when I was done and told me that I needed to stay relevant in life. It clicked for me. If you step away from things for a long enough time, you start to lose your place.

I had to still be a part of it. Analyzing football and talking about the sport that I knew on TV and knowing the players I just thought it was a great opportunity. I didn't have rings or big persona. I had to grind. It's something that I continue to put my pedal on. I want to be the best at it.

JIM MILLER
FORMER NFL QB, SIRIUS XM NFL ANALYST
@15MILLER

Sports have always been important for all of us. I am from a family of five. My dad said that it was important for us to enjoy our childhood and had to be involved in something that would occupy our time. My oldest brother was a quarterback at the local high school. He taught me how to throw a football and I just wanted to be like my big brother.

My dad took me to see a Detroit Lions game when I was nine years old. They were playing Tampa Bay. I saw Doug Williams throw a football and I knew that was what I wanted to do. He launched it about 80 yards and I was just amazed. My brother and Doug Williams solidified that quarterback was what I wanted to do and that football was going to be my sport. I knew when I played in ninth grade and started getting letters recruiting me to play college football that it was going to be an avenue for me to attend college and get a degree. My parents were pretty much broke after putting my older siblings through college.

I wanted to continue being around the game because I didn't get to go out on my own terms. I signed with the New York Giants and blew out my hip. The doctors told me that I was done. I didn't reach all of the goals that I wanted to reach but I did enjoy my 12 years in the NFL.

I love football; I love talking about it with anybody. I am kind of a junkie and SiriusXM NFL allows me to get my football fix. I can stay connected with the relationships that I have developed within the NFL. It's a great comfort zone for me. It's a perfect opportunity for me.

Like every young player, I had dreams of being the next Joe Montana. Not everything goes according to plan. Injuries play a part of it. I had a lot of injuries. For me, I've never reached what I feel was my potential in the NFL. I had extreme highs, extreme lows, I served in all capacities. I grew up, matured and understood my roles on teams. I saw what it took to win on a championship team and how to fit in with a unit that accomplished winning a world championship. I think when I was healthy and playing at a high level, I proved to myself that I could play well and consistently but it wasn't over the long term that I felt I could have been. To me, with the injuries, it was incomplete and I don't feel that I reached my potential.

The thing that I loved the most about football was just winning. The emotions of a win, all of the hard work, everyone coming together from all walks of life, blacks, whites; from an organizational standpoint. When you go through a week's worth of preparation or even season of preparation and then you accomplish your goal, it's earned. It doesn't come easy and takes a great deal of hard work to achieve it. It is a great sport, a team sport and is the ultimate team sport. I will always cherish the effort that it takes and the relationships that it builds throughout the years.

JOHN HARBAUGH
HEAD COACH - BALTIMORE RAVENS
WWW.BALTIMORERAVENS.COM

For me, it probably took a while until my dad had me coach at Western Michigan. I tell myself that but probably the truth is growing up there might not have been another choice. My dad was coaching and we were playing sports. We were around players all of the time. He would have all of the players, their wives or girlfriends at the house all of the time for dinner. It was part of our life, part of our family. It was like the family business.

Football is tough. It is demanding. It creates adversity in our lives. You get knocked down in football. You get knocked down and get back up. You line back up and sometimes the person across from you is bigger, stronger and faster but you still have to get back in there. To me that's one of the great things about football.

It's an equal opportunity sport. It's an equal opportunity endeavor. It may be one of the last true meritocracies in society. You go out there and it's really what you do, what you accomplish. You earn your own way in football. It doesn't matter what neighborhood you come from, what your socio-economic background is, what you look like, it doesn't matter. When you put the helmet on, you're a football player. How you do, is how you do. I feel that's one of the great things about sports in general, but especially about football.

DEONE BUCANNON

NFL DEFENSIVE BACK - ARIZONA CARDINALS

@DEONEBUCANNON20

I was born with this love for the game. It wasn't just one day that I just said 'I love football.' That's just how it always was. When I watched it as a little kid, that's what I told my mom and dad that I wanted to do. I remember the day. We were walking, I was a little kid and they were playing football on the street. I saw them playing football and I said 'that's what I have to do.' I promise you, I was really small.

Ever since then, I told my dad and he said that it was fine but I had to have a plan B. It's funny, when you get to high school it's your plan B but when you get to college, it's your plan A and B. Then once you go through college, it's your plan A. It's time to reach for your dreams. It's a blessing for that to happen. It's rare but it's a big deal for me to get my degree.

I understand that I won't play football for the rest of my life but at the same time, it's a privilege to get the opportunity to play this game that I love. The best that I could tell you was that it's a pleasure to play this game.

WELDON BROWN

CFL Defensive Back - Saskatchewan Roughriders
@WeldonBrown

I had been playing football since I was seven-years old. A lot of my friends played basketball, football, and baseball. I started with baseball. That was the first sport I ever played. I had a passion for the game and was pretty good. I watched Deion Sanders and a couple of other guys during the Cowboys' era in the '90s. Since then my passion[for football] grew.

I was about to quit football in junior high and concentrate on basketball. Basketball was my passion but I didn't get the size. A guy that was in my seventh-grade class didn't know I played football and teased me about being too skinny to play football. That drew me out there to prove myself. Since seventh grade, I've been ballin' ever since.

I played running back and defensive back in high school, but mainly running back. If they needed me to stop somebody I played DB. I just developed a passion. I had a goal of making it professionally. It was the NBA, but once I took on football that remained my main goal. One thing that has kept me has been God keeping me healthy and surrounding me with the right people. Some of my mentors growing up, mainly my coaches and people around the community and around the church develop me to be a professional.

My main goal going to college was to graduate and be a kinesiology major. That didn't work out for me but my wife is, so I still managed to get that under my belt some kind of way. I really wanted to graduate in three years and go pro, but sometimes things don't work out the way you expect them to work. Another thing that kept me involved was my work ethic. I've seen other guys they don't work as hard or they don't want it more than me. I feel like I want it more than everyone no matter where I go. I have the passion. It's been there since I was seven-years old as far as wanting to be the best in everything I do. I have a great support system as well who kept me grounded.

That's really what gave me the edge. I've had setbacks since little league. When I was playing basketball or football, I felt like I worked harder than anyone else and I felt like I was the best player. The coaches may give a trophy to someone they feel deserved it. I've thrown away trophies because I didn't get the recognition that I deserved. By that happening, that got me stronger for the next phase because I wanted to prove to people at the next level, from little league to junior high, then on to high school. My freshman year, the guys that I played with were guys I had been playing ball with since I was seven-years old. They got moved up to varsity and I didn't. I got put on the backburner. They also brought one of the running backs in our area and moved him up to varsity instead of me.

I still played my position and was always a team player. I just felt like I would be good no matter where they put me. After my freshman year, I worked exceptionally hard that summer because the talk around the town was that our football team wouldn't be very good. I remember thinking to myself, 'what are they talking about? I'm right here.' I ran to practice, I ran to weightlifting in the summer time. I also worked out with the varsity guys. I hadn't missed a workout since I've been playing. I know that faith without work is dead and I worked exceptionally hard. My first time carrying the football that season, people started missing the bus just so they could see me practice and I kid you not, I never hit the ground in high school, but I had to find my way in college.

It was like I wasn't chosen again when they didn't put me at running back. My first collegiate game was against the Florida Gators. They gave me one run and one reception. One thing led to another and I switched positions. So I just took on the role of just being on that island by myself playing cornerback. I'm still learning the position as far as being a defensive back because I was playing running back in high school. It's been by God's grace that I'm still playing.

Coming into college I was one of 24 recruits and I'm the only one still playing. Many lose their passion and a lot of guys weren't focused on their education and dropped out because they couldn't get the grades, some had selfish attitudes and others moved on and transferred. My experience in high school having to wait my turn really prepared me for what I faced in college. When it was my turn to step up, I was able to get the job done. I made sure I got good grades; I made sure I practiced hard. I stayed humble and worked really hard so that I couldn't be denied.

HIROKO JOLLEY

OWNER & OFFENSIVE LINEMAN - UTAH FALCONZ
WWW.UTAHFALCONZ.COM - @UTAHFALCONZ
MASCOT MIRACLES FOUNDATION

I had two sisters growing up and a younger brother. My dad raised us to not throw like a girl and I always had that mentality. When I was 11 years old, there was this movie called The Quarterback Princess. It was about a girl that went to high school, became a quarterback and the homecoming queen. I didn't realize that it was a true story. I always had that vision in my head. I wanted to play football; be her and just like her. That's where the passion came from. I started playing around 2010 and after about 2 1/2 or 3 years of playing, I saw a lot of things that could be done differently playing. I wanted to be more involved with it. When the team started falling apart, I offered to buy the team a few times because it was struggling. I decided to start my own team and it took off from there.

I think there will be a point where I am no longer playing and I'll just be an owner but once you get that taste of playing, you just have to play. That drive is just in there; lining up and hitting someone that is bigger than you, taller than you, it's a rush. It's something that's really satisfying. It helps me to connect with my team and gives me better perspective as an owner as far as what is going on. I can understand what they feel and think, how the coaches interact.

I can't imagine my life without football. It drives my family crazy, but they put up with it. I could eat, sleep and breathe football 24/7.

MARCUS WOODSON

DEFENSIVE BACK COACH - FRESNO STATE UNIVERSITY
WWW.GOBULLDOGS.COM - @DOGSWAGGER_FS

I grew up in a town called Moss Point, Mississippi. Football is everything. Everybody played football and that was my dream coming up -- to be a professional football player. It was my number one love. Unfortunately I suffered some injuries throughout my college career that got me involved with coaching. But you know what? If I could do it again, I wouldn't change a thing.

I love doing what I'm doing. It allows me to give back. Ever since I've been coaching, I haven't worked a day in my life. It's something I have a passion for and it's not work because it's something that I love doing. To be able to have a job and not work a day in your life is something that is a pleasure for me to be a part of.

For my life, it's faith, family and football and that's it. Other than my family and my faith, nothing comes before football. It's pretty much all I know, all I've been around all my life. The things that I've learned throughout playing and coaching have all made me a better man. There's nothing that I would change. Football is something I couldn't see myself not being associated with. I can't be a fan; I have to be involved in some way. Obviously being a coach gave me the best opportunity to stay as close to the game as possible without being a player.

DON WILLIAMS
HEAD COACH - BOSTON RENEGADES
WWW.BOSTONRENEGADESFOOTBALL.COM - @GORENEGADES

I love the game of football. I used to own and coach a men's semi-pro team. When I found out about the Boston Militia that was starting up, I had a friend that was coaching with the Militia, and I wanted to take that chance and coach the Women's game. The reason why I took that chance is because at the time the Militia had 3 ex-NFL coaches on the staff and if I wanted to get better as a coach, it would be in my best benefit to join that staff and test myself, while learning from guys that have made it and done it at the highest level. I knew if I couldn't cut it there, then maybe I should leave coaching alone. So that challenge is what initially drew me in. I just wanted to be a better coach. So as I got into the women's game, I realized that once they snapped on that helmet and put on those shoulder pads, they became football players and not just women. I'm glad to say that I coach football players.

I can't get enough of football and I will watch it on every level. I have 2 sons that play in college, one at Trinity and the other at Elmhurst. I just love the game; so anytime I can be around it, I'm at peace. I can say that I always knew that football would be my career in some way, shape, form or fashion. I'm an ex-military guy, so I love the structure of the game. I love everything that comes with the sport of football.

The mark I hope to leave on the game, especially on women, is that they've learned and understand the game, now they want to give back to the game, which keeps building the women's game. That's ultimately what we're trying to do here with the Boston Renegades; we're trying to build women's sports. The first thing people think when you say 'women's football', is the lingerie league. So, I just hope that when it's all said and done, that they can say that Coach Williams taught me the game and therefore I have a true love and passion now for football that wasn't there before.

NASIRA JOHNSON
RUNNING BACK - ATLANTA STEAM (LFL)
WWW.LFLUS.COM/ATLANTASTEAM · @J_NASIRA

I was at the gym playing basketball and one of the girls that played on the New Jersey Titans came in with her pads on, just the bottoms. I asked her about it and she suggested that I try it. I went to practice and I haven't looked back since. I used to play as a kid, growing up in an urban area. The boys and me would play two-hand touch in the street or in a vacant lot. In high school, I worked out with the football team in the summer to get me prepared for basketball. It wasn't something that was distant in my life so to speak. I never thought that it would be as fun as it is though.

I love everything about the game. I can't sit here and name one particular thing that stands out. From the moment that I step into the arena, driving to the arena, the field, entering the arena, going into the locker room, getting taped, stepping out on the field for pregame warm-ups, to kickoff, everything, every moment, every second is exciting to me. That's something that I can't even explain. I wonder if that is the same feeling that the guys get.

I would want people to say that I was one of the best running backs that ever played this game period. As far as the skill level, she could do the same thing that Barry Sanders does, the same that Adrian Peterson does. It would be a goal to be compared to the great running backs in the NFL as far as the skill set. I want Nasira Johnson to be about breaking barriers. She is small, fearless, consistent, and courageous. I want my legacy to stand out in that aspect.

BRENTON SUMLER

LIFE SKILLS COORDINATOR - LOUISIANA STATE UNIVERSITY

WWW.LSUSPORTS.NET

Growing up in a small town in Arkansas, we used to play this game called 'Kill the Man with the Ball'. It was basically a game where you had to run from one end of the field to the other without getting tackled. It was just you against everybody else. And whoever was able to make it from one end to the other, was typically thought of as 'the man' in the neighborhood. So, growing up I saw some of the guys that were able to do that and they went on to be great football players at the high school level. Now, I grew up playing baseball. I was a hell of a baseball player. This one particular day that people were calling me out, I believe I was about 8 or 9 years old. The guys out there were saying 'yeah, you're good on the baseball field, but can you come out here and do the same thing?' So the first time I touched the ball, this girl named 'Big Ackee' laid me out. She was probably about 6'4 200lbs out there playing with the boys. Obviously that embarrassed me so the next time I got the ball, I ran over her and everybody else. And that feeling of overcoming 'this big monster' after getting embarrassed made me believe that I could do this for the rest of my life. So, I ended up loving football from that point on and ended up going to college at Arkansas-Pine Bluff and doing pretty decent.

I can't imagine my life without football. Keep in mind, I started off as a baseball guy. I could tell you about any player, team, history or whatever. But football captivated me and has been such a big part of who I am today. Because a lot of the relationships I've built, a lot of the friendships and a lot of the people I've met has been because of the game of football. And even though I got a 'late' start, I didn't start playing organized ball until the 7th grade, once I put on that helmet and those shoulder pads, I just couldn't see myself without it. I mean, everyone has had that experience of his or her first fall season, smelling the fresh cut grass, you kind of go through a small bit of depression when the season is over. That just lets you know that this is something that you just can't live without. Even though I don't play anymore, I'm still heavily involved in it from stats, to players, to teams, to what I do today as a career. Saturdays and Sundays in my household, I'm pretty much a hermit. I just sit there and watch football all day and night.

ELVIS JOSEPH

RUNNING BACKS COACH - SOUTHERN UNIVERSITY
WWW.GOJAGSPORTS.COM - @SOUTHERNU_BR

As a kid, I watched my big brother play the game and I've always been a big fan of the game. I mean, whenever we had free time, we always played football. Initially in the neighborhood it was a way to pass the time. When it was football season, we played football. When it was basketball season, we played basketball and so on and so forth. But my love was always football. I always had a dream of playing at the highest level. When I was in school, all I could think about was being on the football field.

I came from a rough beginning. When I was in high school, I was hanging with a bad group of guys. My high school coach pulled me to the side and forced me to make a decision. He told me that I either hang with those guys, or play football. So I made that decision to play football and as a result, I had to cut a lot of the friendships I had at the time because it was that important to me. Looking back on it today, I can honestly say that it was a great decision.

It's the camaraderie, the brotherhood, meeting good friends as well as the discipline instilled in me, is what I really love about football. At different stages in life, you learn to fall in love and you learn to appreciate it more. When I was in high school, I loved the attention, the newspaper articles, the bands; I loved all of the elements that came with it. But once I got to college and I started to mature, it became more about the relationships you were building. It became about growing as an individual; the game forces you to become organized; forces you to be great in the time management department, and it molded me into the man I am today.

Football really saved me from the streets of New Orleans. Growing up there, it was a lot of tough decisions you have to make and it's very easy to turn a go down the wrong path. I had a big brother, who passed away, that I loved to death. He was a tremendous athlete in both football and basketball, but the streets got the best of him and he died from a drug overdose. So it really saved me from making bad decisions because, that was the crowd I was raised around. Making that decision to focus on football also helped me focus on my academics. Those two went hand-in-hand because in order to participate in football, I had to do right in the classroom with my grades.

KYRIES HEBERT
DEFENSIVE BACK - MONTREAL ALOUETTES
WWW.KYCARESFOUNDATION.ORG - @KYHEBERT

Football was really big in the culture where I grew up. All of my big cousins, family members, friends and basically everyone in the neighborhood played football. There wasn't much to do. There wasn't a YMCA, or a Rec Center, so people just kind of played what was in season...and it was always football season where I grew up. In high school, football was the biggest thing in town. Those guys were celebrities. I had a big cousin who played ball that I looked up to and said "One day, I wanna be like him". I'd go to the games and instead of watching the game, I'd be down in the bleachers playing football.

In 6th grade I made up my mind that I wanted to be a pro athlete. I really didn't know what it was going to take to get there. I remember in 5th grade doing the percentages of those that actually set that goal (making it to the NFL), and those who actually achieved that goal. And I remember saying, "Wow, there's going to be 99.3% of people watching me do what I want to do". So even then as a kid, I knew that it wasn't going to be easy attaining that goal, but I was ready for the challenge.

I love the physicality of the game. I feel that's the one word that sums up my passion, love, my appreciation for the game and it all comes down to physicality. Growing up in the projects, you didn't get the same rules and the same structure that you would get in the suburbs or somewhere else. So, where I was from, physicality in a young man wasn't something that was frowned upon, it was actually encouraged. If you wanted to hold your own, didn't want to be considered soft or get pushed around, you had to be physical.

When it is all said and done, I want it to be known that I played the game with a passion that was matched by no one else's. I play with a deep love and appreciation for the game. I also wasn't the type of player to back down from anything. I remember playing for the Cincinnati Bengals, we were playing the Dallas Cowboys in Dallas. At that time, the 4-man wedge was legal and three 300lb guys in the way on the kickoff return; and at the time, I'm 225lbs. My job was to destroy that wedge. My friends and family was there at the game...they could've had 8 guys in that wedge, they weren't going to stop me. I ran as fast as a I could, ran as hard as I could and it didn't matter what was going to happen once that collision was made. I would've rather die than to lose to those guys on that play. THAT'S me on a football field.

JASON NEGRO
Head Coach - St. John Bosco Prep HS (CA
WWW.BOSCOFOOTBALL.COM - @BoscoFootball

I think what initially drew me into the game of football was the camaraderie that you have with the players and relationships that grew out of the game. It was something totally unique and something that you sort of went through all together; you struggled and it was difficult, just a way for you to get close with the friends you had in your neighborhood.

You know it's funny because for me, I went through high school playing football and baseball, then playing a little bit of college baseball; I went that route coming out of high school. I was a little bit more talented in baseball, so I went that route and played a few years. And honestly, while I was continuing my college education, I was working for the LA Unified School District and I started coaching the Junior All-American 7/8-year-old football team with a friend of mine. It was SO much fun and so exciting to get the opportunity to work with those guys, that I decided to change my major halfway through college, and work to become a high school teacher and a coach.

I just think that the competitive nature of the game is what I love the most about it. There are so many moving parts. You're talking about 22 players on the field at one time; you try to get 11 players to work in unison at one time to carry out a game plan that you spent all week trying to put in. It's really exciting and satisfying, each and every week. I think that's the biggest thing, to be able to put so much time and so much effort into something, and then to see the execution lay out in front of you underneath the bright lights of Friday night is probably the most rewarding thing.

We hope that the imprint we have on the players is that there was a lot of respect shown and that we did things the right way. I hope that they see that we tried to teach the bigger life skills in a smaller environment. That's the biggest thing that I want to try and get out of it and I hope that the players that we've had the opportunity to coach here, see when they're in their lives. Hopefully that the lessons and things we tried to teach them in school, and with such young and impressionable minds, they're able to draw upon those later in life and be a better person.

John Lambourne
Head Coach - Bingham High School (UT
www.binghamminers.org - @bingham_miners

Man, you're asking me to go back a long way (laughs), but I think I really did like the physical nature of it, and of course the competitiveness of the game. I didn't really know much about it at the time, other than what I saw on TV. My dad took me to sign up, so I did. I sort of fell into the game (coaching) long term as I initially started out more geared toward basketball than football. The basketball coach at the school that I started at, he knew that I played football and suggested that I give it a try at the school, so he recommended me to the Head Coach and we just sort of took off from there. So there wasn't really a point where I made that decision. But when it came to coaching just in general, I do remember having the thought that I loved being a student-athlete, so why not be a coach-teacher.

I think it's the competition and the physical nature of the game that I love the most. I think young men like to be physical. But I don't think they'll just hammer on each other, if there wasn't a scoreboard. The competition is a big part of our society and that's why people tend to gravitate toward the game. I often say that in my health classes that even with goal setting, create a scoreboard because look all of the people that come to a football game just to watch, because of the scoreboard. If you take the scoreboard away, they wouldn't do it…they wouldn't watch it.

All I want people to know about me is that I cared, and I competed. It's really hard because, we do try to use football as a means to help kids and bring them along and teach lessons. Those lessons don't exist if we're not competing. We're out here in Utah, with the heavy LDS denomination, we have something we call 'Church Ball' and part of the emphasis of that is to develop and promote sportsmanship. Well, if there's no scoreboard, nobody cares who wins and you're not going to have a problem with sportsmanship! However, when you throw that element of scoring and competing into the equation, then you're going to have problems. And that is where the overcoming obstacles and learning process takes place. I have to say that my staff does a great job with the kids and it just shows how much you really care about the kids you work with, how much you miss them when they're gone and how much you want them to capture something from the experience. But I also think we have to lead out in the 'competing' part. Because 'competing' requires that we come to work everyday, strive to be better everyday and we challenge each other and hold each other accountable for everything we do. So, I really think football and life is a good marriage!

Lastly, football is a serious grind and you say to yourself everyday "Man what am I doing and how long can I do it?" And then you get to Friday night with the guys and it makes it all worth it. It's the build up prior to the game that's really, pretty cool. I feel like this, I'm 53 years old, and I know so many people, so many of my friends and other people I associate with, that would love to do what I'm doing right now; so the grind of everything you do as a coach, the gratitude and reward comes back to you once you step out there on the field and get that swift reminder of why you're doing what you're doing in the first place! I know it's just high school football, but to us, it's much more than that. It's our passion.

CHRIS FORE

SPECIAL TEAMS COORDINATOR - OAK HILLS HS (CA)
WWW.COACHFORE.ORG - WWW.EIGHTLACES.ORG
@COACHFORE

I grew up in a small town in California of about 45,000 people. My dad played football at the local high school. My uncle was a star at the local high school, homecoming king and president, and football captain. So for me, I grew up in an environment where if you were a boy in this town and if your name was Fore in this town, you wanted to play football. That's just the environment I grew up in going to those games every Friday night with my dad; after the game hanging out until the fields cleared, the lights were on still and playing catch with him pretending I was one of those former Warriors, those football players I just saw play. We'd reenact the plays right after the game right on the field and I loved that, I lived for those Friday nights when I was growing up as a kid. It just kind of naturally drew me in, "Hey I'm going to one day be like this too, I'm going to play football here." You go downtown and see kids from the high school in line at the grocery store and you'd ask them for autographs, those kids were gods to you. It was a great environment to grow up in for football.

I think what captivated me as a young boy when I looked at the game on the field, was a group of people all coming together at one time for one purpose and that was to score. I always liked the offensive side for some reason, even as a little kid. It was the whole concept of a group of people coming together, working as a team, to do everything they could to score a touchdown. Even as a young kid, to see the struggle that was, and how they had to overcome it or fight through it, and I remember sitting there with my dad and he would tell me, "It's not over yet, the game's not over." There's a lot of times where if my team was down by a couple touchdowns, there was always that hope that my guys can come back, battle back and win this thing. That environment where you have a stadium full of people cheering for those boys on the field, football gives you this sense that "we can do it" as a community. We can do it, we can beat these guys, and we can come together right now as a group of people and overcome something.

My story's a little unique. I played two years of high school football and then, coming home one night from a church youth group, I was in a car accident. My friend, a teammate of mine who played at the high school, he was driving and lost control of the vehicle. He got his license that morning, so as an inexperienced driver, we hit a telephone pole. He was killed on impact, my left leg was really destroyed and they told my mom they would have to amputate from the knee. Through the grace of God, I was able to keep my entire leg, but I went through five surgeries over the next month. I had rods and pins inserted.

So my junior year, I was in a wheelchair for the entire football season. When something you wanted so bad your entire life, being out there under those Friday night lights playing varsity football is taken away, that was a very tough thing for me to deal with obviously. For me being in that wheelchair on the sideline was like, "okay now what can I give to my team now?" Actually Junior Seau grew up near me down here in Southern California, and a friend of mine knew him. And Junior called me after this accident right in the middle of his training camp in 1992 when he was a pretty big deal here in San Diego, and he encouraged me and told me you've got to find a way to contribute to your team. He said it doesn't matter if you're in a wheelchair, on crutches, or if you're the star quarterback, everybody's a part of that team. He told me about an injury he had at USC that kept him on the sidelines and that was the first time he had ever been on the sidelines and a football coach told him, "Hey you've got to contribute, you are a part of this team." So he called me to encourage me to find a way to contribute and I never really thought I could. How am I supposed to contribute to this game of football, to this team from the sideline? But what I learned over that year was that I did have something to contribute, and that was some knowledge of the game that I had and the passion for the game that I had to encourage and inspire my brothers, my teammates who were playing. That's when I knew, even sitting in a wheelchair I knew, I'm looking at the game through a different light for the first time ever and that's when I knew I want to do this for the rest of my life.

Then my senior year when I was coming back I broke my foot the first day of spring practice. I went back against doctor's orders and that was it. They said you're totally done now. My head coach gave me an opportunity to stay on his staff and coach the freshmen that year so as a senior in high school, I was coaching the freshmen kids and stayed in touch with my high school teammates and they voted me most inspirational player on the team. Through that car accident I found a calling into coaching that I wanted to use this game to encourage and inspire young men in their lives.

I would like to think people would say that Coach Fore used this game of football to encourage and inspire men to put it succinctly. Nothing is better than hearing from a former player who reaches out to say, "Coach thank you for what you did for me back then because now I just encountered this in life and you helped to make me a better person and I was able to overcome it."

JERRY ANGELO

FORMER COLLEGE & CFL COACH, FMR NFL GENERAL MANAGER
WWW.SCOUTINGACADEMY.COM · @REALJERRYANGELO

Well that was pretty easy for me as my dad was a high school football coach, so I grew up in football. I started at a very young age and stayed with it. For me it was what I was going to do for the rest of my life, I never really thought of anything else. I grew up in a football environment, played football all my life, and was very fortunate to be around some great coaches starting with my dad. My coaches were my role models.I never saw life being anything but football or having football in it in some capacity.

I love the camaraderie of the locker room, coming together as a team. I've been very fortunate to be a part of some great teams; something bigger than ourselves. That really was something that I always cherished; when I look back on my good memories, it was a lot of the people I was with, the things we were able to accomplish, and some of the hardships we had to overcome as well. Secondly, just the competitiveness of the game, all that goes into the preparation during the summer, during the spring and when you get to the fall you see it all manifest itself on the field. You just can't underscore the high that you get from playing and it was just always a big part of my life.

Hopefully that in the end you were a good teammate and you made the game a little better based on what you contributed to it.

EMORY HUNT JR.

CEO/Founder & Analyst - Football Gameplan
WWW.FOOTBALLGAMEPLAN.COM - @FBALLGAMEPLAN

I started playing football at 5 years old and instantly fell in love with it. Football is the perfect combination of athleticism, strategy, bonding, anger, grace, poetry, power and speed. It's probably the only game that encompasses all of those traits. Once I started playing, my life became immersed in it. I probably was the only 5 year old that could sit through an entire football game quietly because I was that tuned into it. If I couldn't, by halftime I'd grab my football and go outside to play it. From birthday cakes, toys, video games, trading cards, everything had to be football. I remember being 8 years old buying football magazines when everyone else was getting comic books. Many times I stayed up past my bedtime to watch the old NFL Films segments that came on television at the time. I was captivated by everything about the game.

I was a very focused and determined kid. I felt that anything that I wanted, if I set my mind to it, I'd get it. So, I knew football was what I wanted to do for a career in some form or fashion. As with most kids, once you find something that you're good at, and you get positive reinforcement, you want to continue to do it. Football to me was like candy to a kid or drugs to an addict. I was addicted to the game. I studied the game and it's history. I used to constantly work on my game with my friends in the neighborhood. And my thought process was that if I couldn't make it to then NFL, then I could become a commentator or something. So early on as a teen, that was my plan. I knew as an 8th grader I wanted to major in Broadcasting. As I moved through high school and playing college football was becoming a reality, it was just feeding my passion even more and I poured more into it. Unfortunately after my freshman season at the University of Louisiana my career was cut short because of a knee injury – same knee that I injured as a high school sophomore – I was devastated. I planned my entire life for everything that happened in it, but didn't plan for the 'what if's.' I remember crying in my dorm room not knowing what the hell to do with my life. But we had an awesome coaching staff at UL and the coaches kept me around the program in many different roles and that experience helped me become a better student of the game, breaking down film from an evaluation and scouting standpoint. At that point, it actually piqued my interest in coaching – which I ended up doing after college at my old high school in New Orleans – and helped grow my football knowledge, introducing me to another side of the game in the process. I felt like that gave me purpose once again.

Once I got out of college I went back and coached at my old high school, McMain, in New Orleans. I absolutely loved it! I wanted to coach there forever but I had people around me constantly telling me that "I should get a real job" and "You didn't go to college to become a high school coach." I also realized that I didn't particularly want to be a teacher, I just wanted to coach football. So I left and jumped into corporate America. I became this Sales Representative/Recruiter for a company. I had absolutely zero interest in the product I was selling and knew nothing about it...but I was really good at it. Go figure! So good at it that I was winning numerous awards for being one of the best in the company. This was a company that was well over 10,000 employees. Like any love or passion, if you try to stay away from it, it has a unique way of pulling back in it. The tipping point was in 2005 when I was coming back from another award banquet in San Diego. I just won an award for being the top recruiter in the company and on the flight back, I'm sitting there with this big trophy and everyone is saying 'great job, that's awesome!' The only thing I could think of was that this isn't a Lombardi, a Heisman, a National Championship crystal football. If it wasn't dealing with football, it didn't matter to me. I wanted back into the game because it was constantly on my mind. That started the ball rolling and in 2007, Football Gameplan was born.

I may be biased, but hands down, football is the best sport on the planet. It's fantastic in every form: playing, watching and storytelling. There's nothing like the smell of the grass, the feeling of anxiousness you get right before the ball is snapped, the roar of the crowd after a big hit or big play, all of those things tend to draw you in more. I love everything about the game but if I had to choose what was particularly important to me, it would have to be the competition and the camaraderie. Football is one of those show-and-prove it type of sports. Being a competitive kid, I hated losing in anything I was doing because losing, to me, meant ridicule from people and I never wanted to have to deal with that. The game became a chance to see how good you were verses an individual on every play. It also was a way to compete against yourself and that fueled me as a kid and as a young adult.

The relationships are another part of the game that I truly love. I'm really close with a lot of the guys I played ball with at every level from little league to high school to college. I find that you even have a unique bond with guys that you don't even know personally but when you find out one another played ball, you tend to become cool. I guess because you both have relatable and common experiences that bonds you. You can say that with any sport, but I think with football having that physical component, it makes it unique and you recognize that not many people want to strap on that helmet and take a hit, so if you did, then that means you're one of the few that wasn't afraid. That's the mutual respect that you see from player to player, coach to coach.

Football Gameplan is my legacy. That's what I want it to be. We cover every league, from the NFL to Women's Tackle Football equally. People are always amazed when they see what we do and they'll say 'wow, you guys cover the smaller levels of college football, CFL, Arena Football, just as much as you guys cover the NFL and major college football.' That's because the game means so much to us. I want people to look back 80-plus years from now and say that Emory Hunt really loved the game and his passion showed through in what he created with Football Gameplan. My whole goal is leaving behind proof that I was here on Earth and since I couldn't leave that impact as a football player, I hope to leave it in the form of Football Gameplan. Hopefully future generations can sit down, turn on their TV and watch Football Gameplan and say 'finally, a place where football makes sense.'

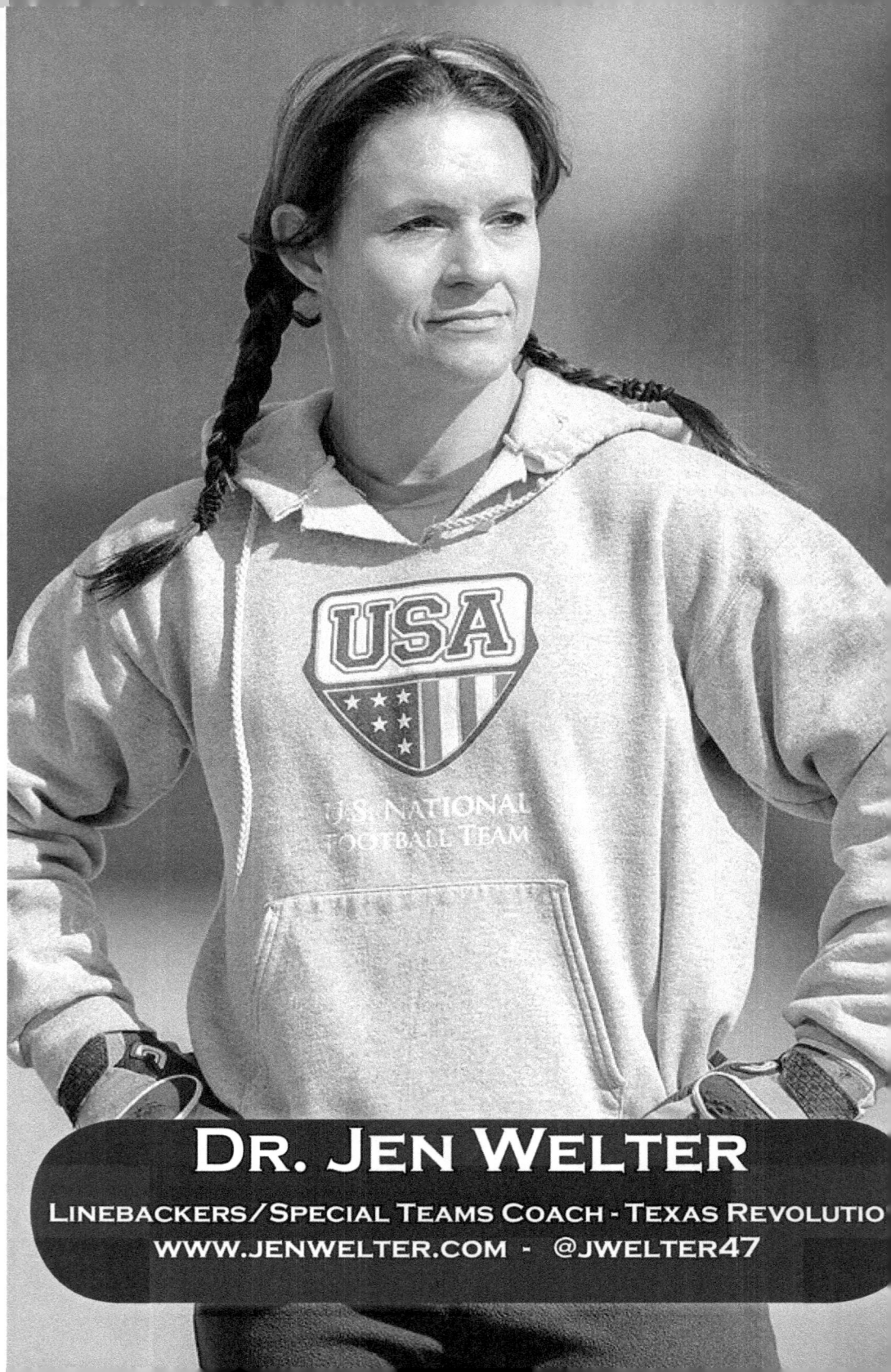

Dr. Jen Welter

Linebackers/Special Teams Coach - Texas Revolutio

www.jenwelter.com - @jwelter47

I grew up in Vero Beach, Florida. The whole city shuts down on Friday nights. Football is like a religion. Everyone goes to the games. I think from the first time I saw it, I fell in love with the sport. My best friends where cheerleaders and they wanted me to be a cheerleader but I was like no, because I can't watch the game.

I was my high school football coach's favorite soccer player because I always took everybody out. Our football team was bad so I would always tell him that he should let me come out for the team. He told me that I was an amazing athlete and that I could help the football team but he asked me not to play. I went to college at Boston College and found rugby and that was the closest that I had gotten to football. I jumped right in. There was no reservation. I thought maybe they would tell me that I was too little but I said that if I don't try, I would regret it for the rest of my life. Once I had the opportunity so I went for it full force.

Most people have the wrong idea of how I ended up with the Texas Revolution. I didn't reach out to them, they reached out to me. The president of the Revolution reached out and said that he wanted to meet with me. It was an interesting situation because he was looking at it from a promotional standpoint. He asked me to come out and go through a day of training camp with the team but I refused because I didn't want to just go through some drills for the camera. That's cheating on the game. I told him that if he wanted to do anything with me that I would have to go in and be just like one of the guys and go through all of the hits and really be a part of the team.

Football is one of the greatest games in the world. It has been such a blessing for me in my life. I think that girls should have the opportunity to play football in the atmosphere and with the support that men get in the game. If women had the opportunity to use the game to further themselves in life, like going to college on scholarship or playing professional football, a lot more of them would play.

I would tell a girl that's playing now that there is a future in women's football. I have seen the sport grow so much. You see stories about girls playing football with boys and doing a really great job. There are some girls doing some amazing things in football.

TIM SHIELDS, ESQ

DEFENSIVE LINE COACH - WASHINGTON UNIVERSITY (MO)
WWW.WASHUFOOTBALL.COM - @SHIELDS3L

The competition initially drew me into the game of football. Just to be able to compete. It was just something that emerged from a love to a passion. It was something that started as a love when I was playing in the backyard, to something I could see myself doing in college. I don't think there's anything like the competition, especially on game day. I played left tackle and I truly like the fact that I could take away a defensive coordinator's best athlete in his defensive end. I've done a lot of different things in my life. I went to law school and passed the bar. And there's a ton of competition in law school. But there's nothing like a Saturday afternoon in the fall on a football field. I think that's why I came back to the game. That fire, which was still burning in me as a player, was still there and I didn't think I'd have that same feeling working in the legal field. And that's how I ended up returning to football as a coach.

I would have to say it was some time back when I was in middle school that I realized I wanted football to be my career. I didn't know in what capacity. I initially wanted to be a coach when I went to college, but that kind of changed when I went to law school and wanted to become an agent. Obviously, I'm back in coaching. I was the meathead in freshman algebra class that drew football plays in my notebook all day long. I knew at a young age that this game just consumed me. Everything else I did outside of football was just that, something I did. Football was my passion. Football was what I loved and thought about 24/7. And I strived to be better at it every single day. It was always a thought in my head that I was going to go play college football, and then I was going to go into coaching.

I hate to continue to belabor the point, but I really love the competition in the game of football. I love the fact of facing someone one-on-one all day. You've worked your entire life; entire offseason just to get to that point and so has your opponent. And you get to find out who's the better football player; who's the tougher guy. For me, that's how I approached everything. When it was the offseason, I wanted to make sure that there wasn't anyone who was going to outwork me. Luckily for me, I had a successful career built around that premise. Honestly, I almost operated in fear during the offseason because I didn't want there to be someone out there, whether it was a defensive end that I was going against or an offensive tackle that I was competing against for playing time, to outwork me. I just wanted to make sure that I was going to be 'the' guy and that is what drove me. And it's really what I love about the game.

I think football is all about relationships. One of the most rewarding things about being a coach is that you can help impact lives. I honestly hope that my impact on the game was that I helped the players I coached become, not only better players, but better students and better men. That's ultimately my goal. I don't know if I'll ever have an impact on a program, or a professional franchise, but ultimately I hope that the impact I'm able to have on young people's lives is what I can leave as my legacy when it's all said and done.

CHELSEA ALT
KICKER/WIDE RECEIVER - MADISON BLAZE
WWW.MADISONBLAZEFOOTBALL.COM - @99PRBSKICKAINT1

174

Just to be completely honest, I was working at a liquor store in Madison, Wisconsin and a girl came into the store with a flyer for, at the time, the Madison Cougars. When I saw the flyer, I initially thought it was for guys. I had just moved to Madison so I was like 'oh, guys playing ball…let me go check out the guys.' And the girl was like 'no, it's women.' I automatically had this puzzled look on my face and asked do women play football? She then said that I should come and check them out. I went to the next practice and that was it; I was hooked. It's funny because it initially started with me trying to go check out guys and ended up with me playing and falling in love with it.

I've always been athletic. I've played soccer, basketball and flag football. So, I've played all of these different sports but full contact football was never an option for me. When it became an option for me, there was absolutely no reason for me not to take it. I would've been foolish to not sign up and play. For me, it was something new and different; it was also something that I was constantly told and assumed that I couldn't do.

I really love the physical part of the game. I used to play soccer and I used to get in trouble all the time, a lot of red and yellow cards from me, because I was too physical. Football allows you to go out there and give it your all and be as physical as you want. Words can't describe the feeling you get playing football. I think it's a place where you get to just be free. I love the game so much that even to this day I'm still heavily involved with helping grow the game in my area. I want to show younger girls that they can do whatever they want to do. Football isn't just a men's sport.

JOE PISARCIK

FORMER NFL & CFL QUARTERBACK

PRESIDENT/CEO OF THE NFL ALUMNI ASSOCIATION

WWW.NFLALUMNI.ORG - @NFLALUMNI

Growing up you're a little influenced by your surroundings and being raised in the Wilkes-Barre/Scranton, Pennsylvania area, back then we played a lot of football virtually year round with a little bit of basketball and baseball thrown in there. Football was very big in my area. I played a lot of it when I was young and everybody was older than me, so I had to toughen up a little bit if I wanted to compete. I truly believe that what you're surrounded by will put you into situations, some good and some bad, but what I was around had a major influence on what I ended up wanting to do with my life.

I was involved in the game for 12 years. Three in the Canadian Football League and 9 years in the NFL. What helped me after was that I wanted to give back. One of my kids, Lindsey, asked me 'Dad, what are you doing to give back to help kids and help the game?' And I didn't really have an answer for her. So about 10-12 years ago, I got involved with the NFL Alumni as a chapter president. I kept on doing that and found out that it is better to give than receive. It just felt good to raise money for kids and most importantly, it was the right thing to do.

I think it's the competition factor and being able to compete against another team is what I love about the game of football. I believe it's the greatest sport in the world because it is the total team concept. If I don't throw a good pass or the linemen doesn't block and the wide receiver doesn't run the correct depth and catches it, if all of those things happen, then we don't have a completed pass. In some other sports like baseball, if you go up to bat and hit a home run, then you just hit a home run. You're doing a lot by yourself. Of course you're being coached how to do it, but a lot of it is a 1-on-1 situation. The total team concept is what makes foot-ball, football. I think that helps you out in life too. You have to work with other people and be a team player. I love football because it's very compet-itive and its values teach you about life, which is something you can take with you forever. You also tend to create a lot of friendships and closeness because of working through these situations.

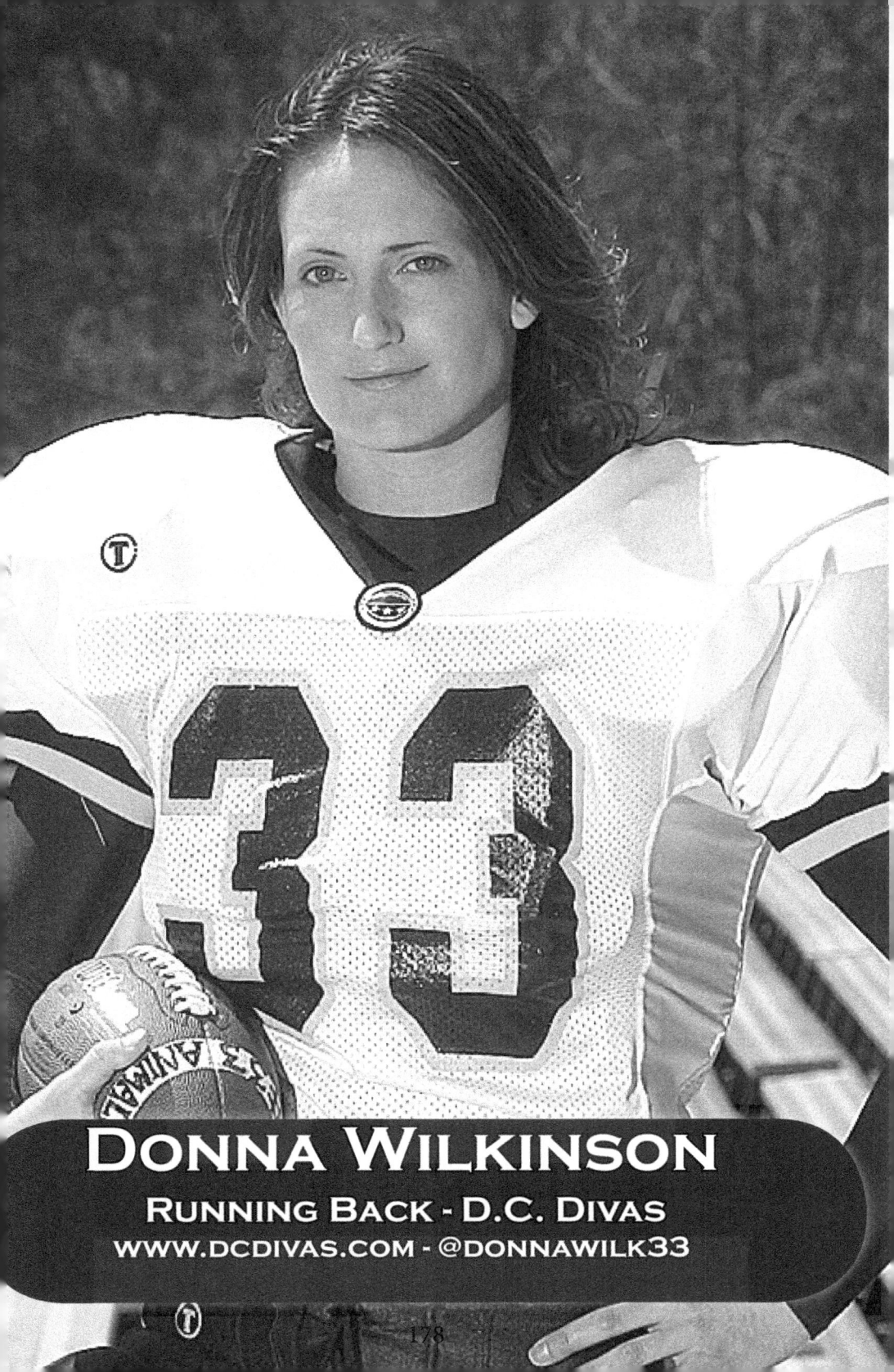

DONNA WILKINSON

RUNNING BACK - D.C. DIVAS
WWW.DCDIVAS.COM - @DONNAWILK33

When I was 5 or 6 years old, we had just moved back from Hawaii and we were staying at my grandparents' house for a short period of time until we got our own place. I remember the Los Angeles Raiders were playing and me telling my grandfather that I wanted to grow up big and strong just like those guys and play football. Obviously my family just laughed it off as me be cute and trying to relate to grandpa. At that moment when I saw the game, it was just natural for me. The game was just beautiful to me. I don't know what it was, but it had me captivated. So that was the first moment when I realized that football was something that I wanted to do.

When it really hit me was in high school. I used to skateboard with the neighborhood boys in the street and throw the football around with them. I remember them getting their pads as they were getting ready to go play organized football and I said to myself, man I want to do that. I was crushed because I was a girl and I couldn't. I was not given an opportunity, as a girl, to play this game. So, by the time I started to play organized sports, I was devastated. I remember saying that I wish I were a boy so that I could play football. At that point I said that I would play every other sport that I can and just used that as my outlet. Basketball, volleyball and softball became my high school sports. I was able to get a scholarship to college for softball. I played 5 sports in college and I was still looking for more when I got out of college. There wasn't really anything I could find that would give me what I needed and wanted. In 2001, the D.C. Divas were recruiting players and I went out to the first meeting. As soon as I put the pads on, everything that I felt since I was 5 years old was right in front of me. I was a little bit angry because it took that long, but I was like there's no going back. There was so much anger that was building in me because of being told that I couldn't play and women couldn't play. Football finally gave me the chance to release all of that pinned up frustration and energy. The whole motivation behind the frustration was to prove to people that women CAN play football and we should be allowed to do so.

Every time I experienced it, I got something more out of it. That kept me coming back and playing for 15 years. I can tell that what I experienced 15 years ago, was different from 7 years ago, and was different from just last season. I constantly was learning something new about the game and about myself. In the beginning, my passion was anger-fueled. The whole 'proving myself' was the motivation. Becoming the leading rusher in the league and rushing for over 1,000 yards, winning numerous awards and having things come back to me that validated my experience also became very important to me.

So at first it was more about ego and definition, but then came a point where I had a major knee injury and the focus then became about finding out whom I am. Sitting out with that knee injury, after playing in the championship game with a torn ACL, put me in a different mindset. If you're always used to being the 'star' and now you're not out there, you're sort of lost and you have to begin to find yourself. And I must say that being away from the field, allowed me to find out more about who I was as a person and a teammate. I used to only lead by example on the field, but being injured allowed me to lead in a different way. I was able to care more about my teammates and about the game itself. It was a big ego-check for me because I realized that the game is much more than individual success, it's more about the team. At that point, I started to focus on how I could become a better teammate, grow the sport, and help the people around me become better players.

I look at it now as an opportunity to bring people together. Football, especially women's football, is a great chance to focus on our similarities and not our differences. I got first hand experience with this by playing with the U.S. National Team. We were playing and practicing against women from Germany, Hungary and others. The funny part is that normally these are countries that may not get along with each other, but we're here together and getting along because of the game of football. You instantly build some sort of sisterhood and camaraderie with one another.

Football is poetry to me. It's art. I'm back in the backfield this year as a running back, and especially from that position, the unison of the offensive line and the running back working together is poetic. Football is so being tied into a moment, that there's nothing else. I think a big part of that is the sport pushes me so hard into a zone. That's a really special place to be. It's like the most sacred place on Earth. There's no place else where you can get that feeling. I also love the adrenaline, the rush, and the calm you get while out there on the field.

I would tell a young female that wants to play football to embrace it, love it and follow it. You have to create an opportunity to do want you want, go after it and stay in your passion. Football is the one thing that I'm extremely passionate about. You can put anything else in front of me and I'll like it and appreciate it, but you won't get me fired up for 2 hours like football does. Hopefully I made a lasting impact on the game. Setting a standard in the process on how the game should be played and what people should look to about playing football as a woman. Changing that perception is huge to me.

CHRIS CANTY

DEFENSIVE LINEMAN - BALTIMORE RAVENS
WWW.CHRISCANTYFOUNDATION.ORG - @CHRISCANTY99

At the crux of it, it's the opportunity to impose your will on another man. There are very few places in this world where you can do that and not go to jail. But the physical nature of the game is something that I enjoy. Again, [it's about] the opportunity to be a part of a brotherhood, to be a part of a team and have 50-plus guys coming together for one common goal. It's something special that happens. I can't really describe it. I can't put it in words, but you know it when you're around it and you feel it. I would definitely say those are the things that just keep you coming back. It's almost like a drug.

MIKE BOBO

HEAD COACH - COLORADO STATE UNIVERSITY

WWW.CSURAMS.COM - @COACHBOBO_CSU

I grew up in a football household. My dad was a high school football coach, his brother, my uncle, coached in high school, college and in the NFL. Initially, I wanted to play for my dad. I wanted to play on Friday nights in the community we lived in, which was a small town in South Georgia. I just wanted to be a part of what he was a part of, and be close to my community.

My dad would always say 'Make sure you do something besides being a football coach.' I kind of listened a little bit (laughs). I was fortunate enough to go play football at the University of Georgia. And it was really near the end of my career there in college that I realized I wanted to coach. I was in the business school there at Georgia, but I just kept thinking back to my dad, the coaches that coached me in college and I wanted to have an impact like those guys had on me. Really all I ever wanted to do was to be a high school coach, but I was fortunate enough that things fell a certain way and I was able to get into the college game. But my main goal was to be a high school coach and have an impact on young kids lives like my dad did.

The number one thing I love about the game of football is the camaraderie you have with your teammates. It is such a team sport where you have to sacrifice for your brother, your teammate in order for you to be successful. Football is not a game where one player can dominate. It takes everybody; from guys that are walk-ons, to scout team guys, the special teamers to the guys that make plays both offensively and defensively. You build such a bond with these guys for what you go through, to play on x-number of Friday nights or x-number of Saturdays. You build such a bond and the camaraderie I had with the guys back when I played, I still have to this day. And then as a coach, it's the same thing. I really love coming to work everyday because of the camaraderie we have here with our staff. We all get along with the families because it's just a bond that we all go through each year, trying to get young guys to do it on the field.

I would want my players to look back and say that I was honest and didn't pull any punches with the players that I coached; that I told them where they stood and what they had to do to get better. I also want them to see that I was a fierce competitor who loved to go out there everyday and compete in anything; from practice to games, it doesn't matter. The message we're constantly preaching is that we got to be honest with each other and trust each other.

At the same time, I want guys that absolutely love the game of football and who loves to compete anytime I put the ball down and say lets go. That's the way we're trying to get these guys to learn because, outside of football, you're going to have to compete for everything in life. That's what makes this country great; it's the competition. This game teaches that and in order to survive, you've got to be the ultimate competitor.

Ralph D. Brown II
Former NFL Defensive Back
College Football Analyst
www.ralphbrownsports.com - @RalphDBrown

I started at 10-years old, but once I got into high school, I was part of a really athletic and talented powerhouse high school and there were a lot of athletes around me. The camaraderie and the family atmosphere combined with the history and tradition that was there, made me really want to be a part of the game and just continue to play as long as I could. It changed my life.

I played for fun and for the love of the game even though I was naturally good. I just really enjoyed what football brought in terms of changing peoples' lives and what I did on the football field. I got the chance to entertain people and have teammates. I wanted to continue doing that all through high school and in college and try to see if I could go to the pros. When I was in the NFL, I always felt like I haven't arrived no matter what I achieved in football. I made sure I stayed humble and I made sure I gave back because I had a lot of mentors in my life. I had people outside of my family that mentored me to be a great player, study the game and pay it forward. That's something I made sure I committed to throughout my life.

I would love for my football epitaph to say that I made sure that I didn't ever abuse the game. I'd love for it to say I was a man that played the game the way it was supposed to be played. When I say that I mean someone who committed a ton of hours in the film room, and that I was someone that did their job. I was someone who treated all players the same despite their varying levels of talent. I would also like for it to say that not only was I willing to learn and be a sponge, but I was also willing to teach as well. I feel like these are the ingredients that enabled me to play as long as I did.

AARON GARCIA
HEAD COACH - LAS VEGAS OUTLAWS
WWW.AFLOUTLAWS.COM - @AFLOUTLAWS

My dad was a high school football coach; he played quarterback and ultimately went into high school coaching. So I was always around the game; always at practice and at the games on Friday nights. It was something that I just really enjoyed from an early age.

I don't know if I ever thought that I'd be a coach but I knew I loved being around the game and everything about it. I remember having birthday parties and my parents would ask me if I wanted to go to a pizza place or take your friends to a movie, and every time the answer always was 'no...I want to go to the football game on Friday night.' My dad didn't let me play tackle football until I was a freshman in high school. I can still remember the first time I got hit and completed the pass it was such a rush. That really stimulated me and I've loved the game ever since. Last year was probably the first time as a player, where I felt as though I didn't have that same fire and it was time to move on. And I wasn't sure if I wanted to get into coaching but then this opportunity with the Las Vegas Outlaws came along so here I am ready to start the next chapter.

There's so much that I love about football like the strategy, but I do think that necessity to be tough, play through pain while standing in the face of danger is another element that I love. Just being in pressure situations and having to make decisions, plays and things that impact everyone around you. Especially at the quarterback position, you have to have the desire to do those things and you have to enjoy that in order to be able to thrive in those situations.

Something my dad always told me before a game when he was the coach, he would just walk up to me and say 'from the heart.' Even now, to this day when we get off the phone, I say from the heart. So I would want people to say that I played the game and lived his life from the heart.

MIKE VAN DIEST

HEAD COACH - CARROLL COLLEGE

WWW.CARROLL.EDU - @FOOTBALLCARROLL

Growing up my dad was my baseball coach and I grew up in a really good baseball community. Baseball was something that I got started in at a very young age. In the 1950s and 1960s growing up just watching football on TV, it's not like it is today where there's virtually a game on every night. We had only one game on Saturday and we had Lindsey Nelson on Sunday right before I went to church that gave the Notre Dame recap. I'd watch that every Sunday before I went to church and I just fell in love with the game of football. The toughness of it, the teamwork of it and I became a huge Alabama and Notre Dame fan. I went to a Catholic grade school and we'd play football at lunchtime, nothing really organized, and we'd have our own uniforms and play teams from across town. I just loved the excitement of football and I loved playing the game.

When I was in high school, I was an undersized kid and wasn't very good. I played for a great high school coach by the name of Cecil Demy. I think he was Vince Lombardi reincarnated as we ran that Packers sweep. The game of football to me in 1950s and 1960s with Woody Hayes, Bear Bryant and Coach Demy was about toughness. Not in the sense of it testing your manhood, but it was a tough game played by tough people. And I didn't see myself as that type of person and wanted to become that type of person so I knew in high school that I wanted to go play college football. I walked on at the University of Wyoming and earned a scholarship. Wyoming was also one of the games we got to see every week living in the Rocky Mountain area. So I just made up my mind that I wanted to go to Wyoming probably as a 7th or 8th grader. Once I played football in college, I just loved it. I just loved the game and the coaches that I had really brought out that passion in me. When I came back home, I was working at a YMCA as a fitness director. I missed the game so much that I called up Fred Akers, who was the head coach at the time at Wyoming, and asked him if I could come back to be a graduate assistant. That's when I knew I wanted to make coaching football my career at the college level.

The strategy of the game is something I love the most. The blocking, tackling and toughness of the game; the Spartan physical characteristics of the game and the teamwork of the game is all a part of my love for it. I just thought it was so great. I'm probably cut from the same cloth as my high school coach running that Packers sweep. In football, everyone is accountable to each other.

Remember, I grew up playing baseball and if you had a great pitcher, you could dominate at the little league level. And in basketball if you had a taller kid on the team, you could dominate in the post at that level also. But in football, it took everybody to make the team successful. I liked challenging myself to see if I was tough enough to play the game. I was an End (Wide Receiver) and I thought that there was nothing better than running a route and catching the football. I also loved the working out aspect of it; loved lifting weights, the running part – I don't know if I particularly loved that part – but I enjoyed the challenge.

I would hope that people would see my passion for the game of football as a coach and as a player. This will be my 40th year as a college coach. To be in it that long, I've seen a lot of changes and been around a lot of players and coaches. I'm still pretty much old school where I think that it's a tough game played by tough people. I just hope the players knew that I loved them, coached them hard and was fair to them. And I want them to have enjoyed the game of football as much as I did. I also hope they know that this wasn't a hobby of mine or something that I just did without putting in any time or effort to help make them the best that they can be. I know how fast the time goes, as football is not a lifetime sport. Football at the high school level and at the college level is pretty well defined for you. Very few go on to play past high school and even fewer go on to play past college. So I just hope the players understood what I was trying to teach and saw how much I loved the game.

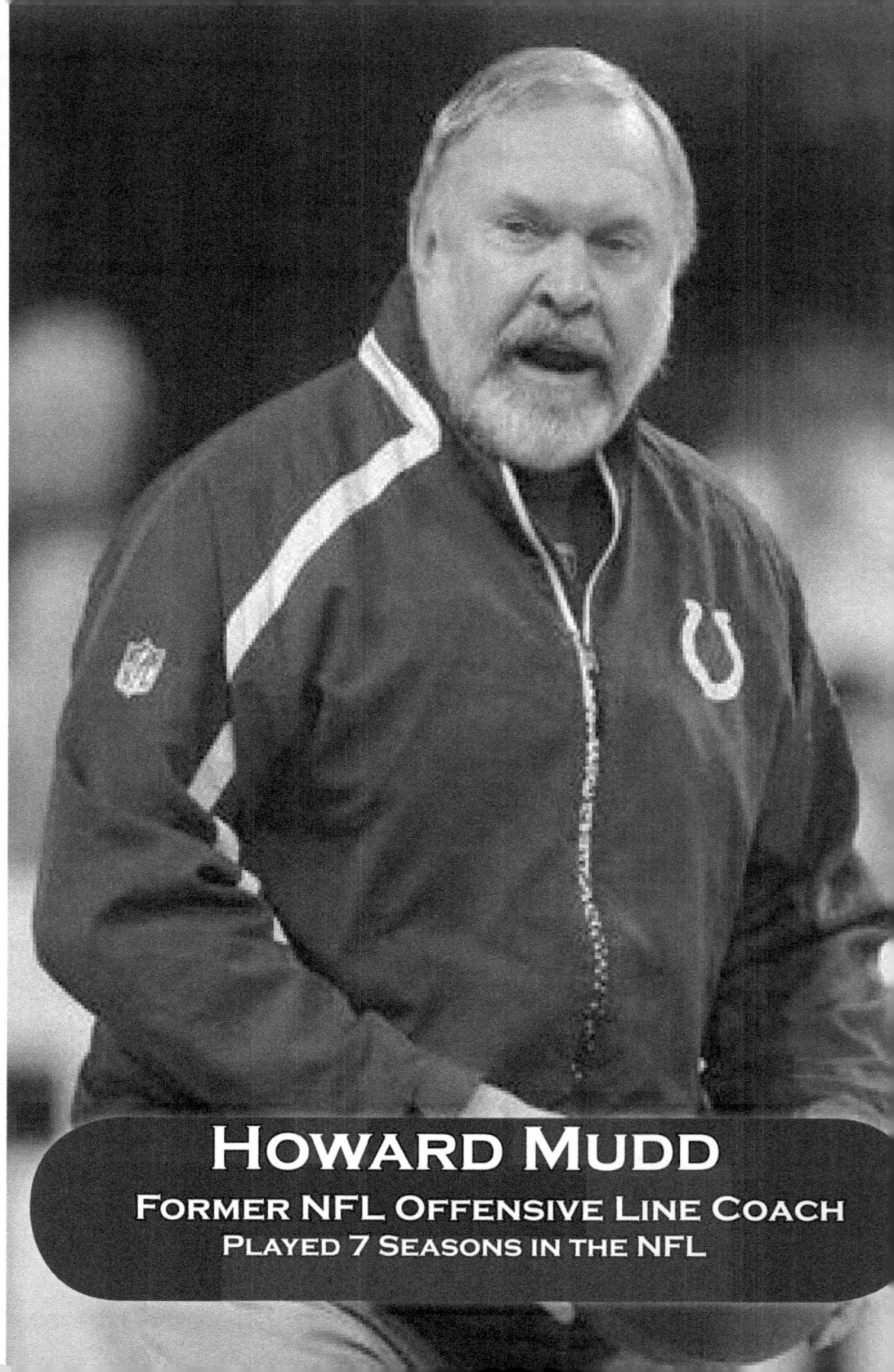

HOWARD MUDD
FORMER NFL OFFENSIVE LINE COACH
PLAYED 7 SEASONS IN THE NFL

God gave me ability. So I knew every place that I went, it would be demonstrated that I had some ability. So the other part, the internal drive comes from the fact that your ego gets rewarded from succeeding, which feeds on its own. So you say to yourself, 'I want to keep doing that because it makes me feel good.' People ingratiate your self-esteem by making a compliment and things like that. That's the playing part of why I wanted to stay involved with the game.

There's nothing that you can measure of the sense of self-satisfaction knowing that you played in the NFL, because there is no better league. To know that you got the chance to play there and play at a high level was pretty satisfying for me. As a coach, imparting that back to and being part of putting that together so other people can do it, is very rewarding. I never felt that I ever went to work. It is hard work, but I never felt as though it was a real job. It was very satisfying in setting a goal, which was teaching players how to play the game better than what they thought they could, and then teaching them the life skills that I learned from the game in hopes that they take that and continue to pass it on.

BOBBY WALLACE

HEAD COACH - UNIVERSITY OF NORTH ALABAMA
WWW.ROARLIONS.COM - @UNAATHLETICS

In elementary school I was kind of forced into participating. I guess I didn't follow football that much; I didn't grow up with it in my early years. And as a fifth grader, the first day I went to practice I finally got it and fell in love with it. It was competition and it was fun. I wasn't a very good loser, which wasn't good, and I hope I was a decent winner. But I think I learned a lot about the adversities you face. I remember I was fortunate enough to be a good athlete, so my team would normally win except the coaches use to always be on the other team to try to help them win and I'd get so frustrated. I just loved the competition and that's where that started. I was successful and I think success helped generate more interest in junior high and high school. I started to get recruited by Mississippi State to play football. I played the other three sports: baseball, track, and basketball, and probably was the best in baseball but in the south, football is king and especially back in those days when college baseball wasn't that big of an issue. So I went for football at Mississippi State and after my years at State, I didn't know what I wanted to do, so the coaches asked me to stay on as a graduate assistant. I didn't have anything better to do and it sounded like an interesting deal and I did it. That's when I fell in love with coaching. It didn't take me long to figure out that's exactly what I wanted to do for a living. I was very fortunate to get a lot of breaks at an early age. I was hired by Pat Dye at East Carolina the next year when I was 22, and the success he had at East Carolina, then at Auburn, he carried me along with him, it was a great experience and ever since that's what I've done.

I've tried to retire twice but I can't do it. Every time I retire, a job that intrigues me opens up and I get back in it. The biggest thing about coaching that always pulls you back is that you miss the relationships with the players, your fellow coaches and the recruiting, that's what I tell players. All players have aspirations to go division one; they can't all do it for various reasons. What I do is try to be sure they understand is that, if they go division two, in fifteen years they are going to get out of it the same things they get out of every division one program in the country; and that's the relationships you have with your teammates and coaches, and that's what sticks with you for a lifetime after you're done playing.

It's the relationships, it's the competing with the team, and it's learning to work with other people. Obviously, you love the individual part of football. I was a running back, receiver, defensive back and I played defensive back in college, so ball skills were always fun for me as well as returning punts. It still goes back to relationships; being in the locker room, joking around, being competitive with other people, having the same goals, obtaining those goals sometimes, not obtaining them and hurting with people. Those are the things that make football such a great team sport. If you are just an individual, I don't think you're going to get as much out of it. You have to be in the team aspect and learn to work with people. That's why I think it's a great sport to help people who don't have a career in football, that go into business. They learn to work with people, set goals and work hard when people are in the off-season and do that extra work it takes to be successful.

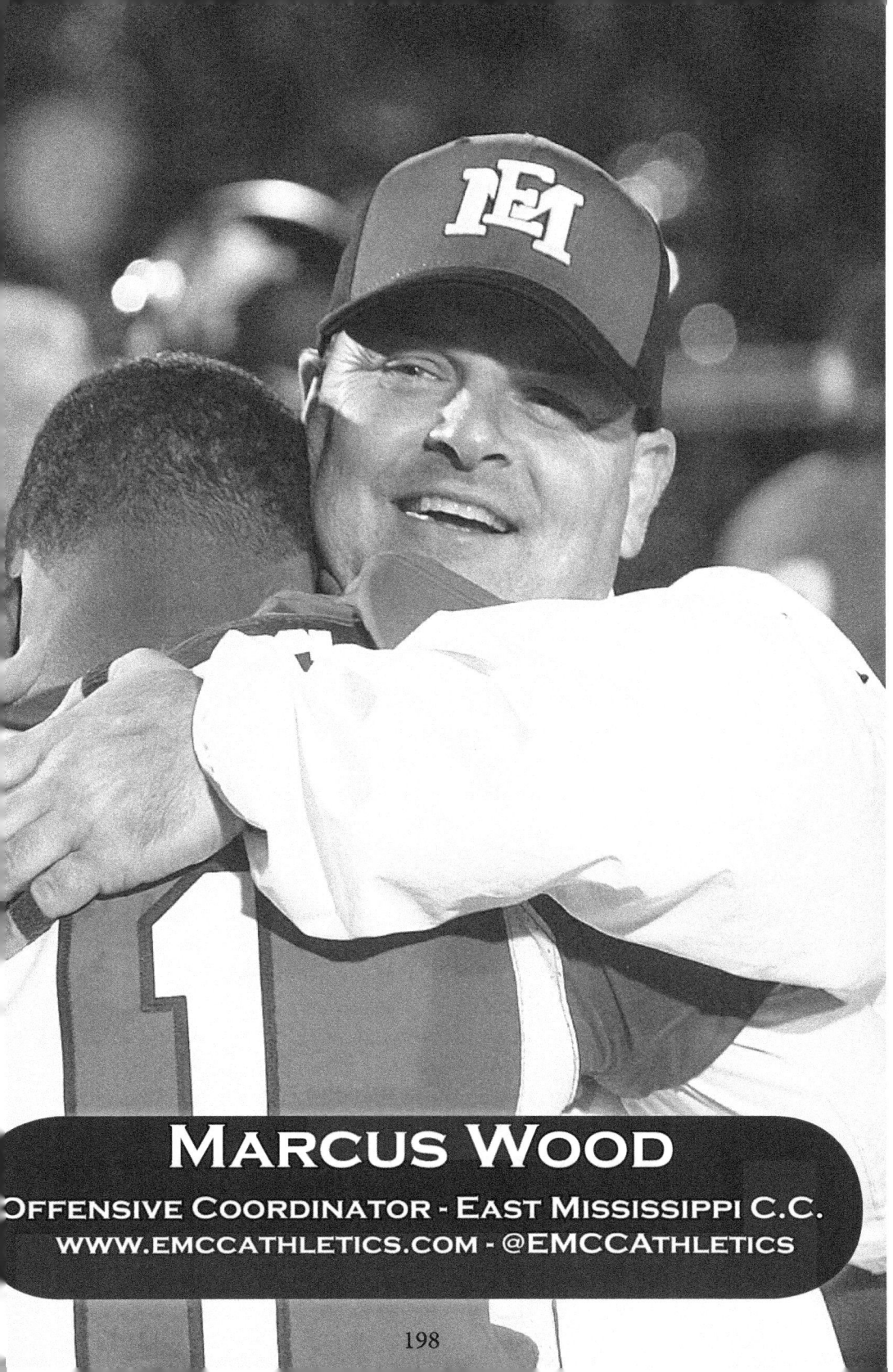

MARCUS WOOD

OFFENSIVE COORDINATOR - EAST MISSISSIPPI C.C.
WWW.EMCCATHLETICS.COM - @EMCCATHLETICS

I grew up in a single-parent family and my brothers all played sports. I played different sports and when I went out for football as a junior high kid in Starkville, Mississippi, it was the camaraderie with the teammates, the relationships and closeness with the guys made me fall in love with the game. I was about 11 or 12 years old and I knew this is what I wanted to be around and what I wanted to do.

I think it's kind of a unique love affair with the game of football. I fell in love with the game when I first started playing and there's no doubting that. I had one brother that was playing college baseball at the time and one that was playing college football. We'd go to ball games at Memphis State back in those days and I can remember going up there and it was everything about it that captivated me; the players and coaches that were there were great to be around, my high school teammates who I was with at the time as well. So I think it was a kind of unique deal during that timeframe of junior high and high school that looped me in completely. And once I started playing, it was something that I really enjoyed and couldn't see myself doing anything else.

I think the closeness with your teammates and coaches is something that I really love about the game. I also love the strategy part of it too; especially being an Offensive Coordinator. I enjoy the breakdowns, the practices, there's not a lot that I don't enjoy about football. There are times I know as a player, that they probably don't enjoy the running or conditioning side of it. I think they endure that because they love the actual game itself so much. So I think as a coach it's the same thing. There may be times where you're working long on the weekends but you look at it as a means to an end; it's a chance to get to those Thursday nights or Saturday afternoon games and get an opportunity to get to see your guys get out there and compete and be around them. The relationships that I have with the players that I coach now are unbelievable. To know what the game means to them in relation to what it means to you is awesome.

I want the players that I've coached to know that I care about them. I have 3 sons of my own and as a single dad, nothing is more important to me than my sons. We talk a lot about your faith and your family at East Mississippi. And I think if you want to leave a legacy, it should be a legacy of care. My players know that if they need anything they can call Coach Wood; if they don't have the answer to something, they know I will try and help them find an answer. My dad died 9 days before I was born, so as a coach you get a chance to impact lives and do good things and I want to make sure that I'm doing that while leaving a legacy of care in the process.

MIKE LEWIS

DEFENSIVE END - LAS VEGAS OUTLAWS
THE LEWIS-HIVE FOUNDATION - @LEWIS2MIKE

My father drew me into the game of football. He played a season down at Grambling State, under the great Eddie Robinson. He was always real adamant about the game of football. I used to sit down and watch all the games with my dad. Every summer before the draft, and before the season, we would go to the gas station and grab a college football magazine, a pro football magazine and also a draft magazine; so we always stayed reading about it. And it was interesting because, it broke down the player's height, weight, where they were from and what the people were saying about the player's talents. That gave me a visual image about football. So every year, if I wasn't thinking about football, I was reading about it. So I would have to thank my father for getting me into the game.

It's the bright lights of football that I really love the most. When those lights are on, the people are watching and it's loud in there; the fans are either with you or against you, it's a rush man! It's the thrill of the chase. It's the challenge of going against somebody that's bigger than you; it's going against somebody that's supposed to be 'all this or all that'. It's the competition; the showing that my best is better than your best. This is what I love the most about the game of football.

I grew up in Auburn Hills, MI. Very near The Palace. I was a huge Detroit Lions fan. I was about 6 or 7 years old and Bennie Blades used to always run around my neighborhood. My little league team used to go to the Silverdome and play. Brett Perriman and Blades used to come out there and talk to us. Those guys were our idols, and that's who we strived to be like. So being able to see Blades' work ethic and having Perriman tell us "don't be afraid to be great". That meant a lot man and those are some of the things you never forget as a kid.

When people look back on my playing days, I want them to be able to say that he didn't cheat the game. I got that (not cheating the game) from Michael Jordan. Even though I'm not on the National Football League level, I'm still out there playing hard each and every time. There's some people that would just rather sit on the side and collect that paycheck. That's not who I am. That's not who I want to be, because at the end of the day, football is going to be football no matter what level you play. I always want to go out and give my all and have people see that I played it at a very high level. The unique part about the game of football is that you don't get to play it forever. It's not even a guaranteed 4 or 5-year career. So, I don't ever want to go out there and cheat the game or have people say that I cheated the game.

I stay in the game because I love everything about it; the weight-lifting, the studying film, the competition, the preparation. I knew that I wanted to play football for the rest of my life during my sophomore year in college. That was the first year that I garnered All-American honors. The funny part about that was, going back to earlier when I talked about getting the magazines every year, I opened up this particular magazine back in 2006, and I saw "Mike Lewis - Adrian". When I saw that, I then said, you know what, I want to do this for the rest of my life. That was the most exciting thing that ever happened to me; just to see myself in that magazine, the same magazine I grew up reading, was an awesome feeling.

I had no idea about the amount of sacrifice, the amount of commitment that those guys at the National Football League level put into this game. Those habits start in college. That's what I would like to teach the younger guys that's coming up in this football world that want to be successful. There's not that much distance between the good and the great. The great ones are the ones who have a routine, they love it and they'll go and 'do it' (workout) even if they don't want to. The good ones, when they don't want to do it, they stop. And coming up in this process myself, I didn't have anybody at Adrian College who made it to the big leagues to guide me. I had to sort of navigate through that journey myself. It's just a bunch of stuff that I had to learn, that I would love to teach the guys coming behind me so that their road would be much easier. That's what I hope my lasting imprint on the game would be; that I helped make the road easier for others.

ERIC BARTEL

Co-Owner & Partner - Financial Coaching LLC
@EricBartel

Family drew me into the game of football. From the time I was born, my dad coached college football for the first 25 years of my life and the last 10 years as a 6A high school football coach in the state of Texas. So, I didn't have an option. I wasn't drawn into it; I was put into it. My first job was a ball boy at UT-Arlington. One of my first memories at UTA was when it was your birthday, the team would dump you in an ice bucket, and you had to stay in there for however many years you were. So, if you were 21 years old, you had to stay in there for 21 seconds. So when I turned 5 years old, they got me in there for 5 seconds. I remember their best player was a cornerback named Tim McKyer and he was turning 20, and I remember my brother and I helping him sneak out of the complex without getting dunked. That was one of my prouder moments in life at the time (laughs). He went on to win Super Bowls with the 49ers and Broncos and every time we talk, he constantly reminds me of that time I helped him get out of the building without getting dunked. But growing up as a coach's kid, I was a ball boy and I was holding the cord of from his headset on the sidelines at UTA, Louisiana Tech and at the University of Houston. So I've just always been around football; football coaches and football players. It's just engrained in my DNA.

I would say that the brotherhood is what I love most about the game. I have a brother, 2 stepbrothers and a half brother. So I have four brothers of my own but the teammates that I played with in high school and in college, there's just a special bond you have with those guys. That bond is forged because you're working out together in that 100-degree heat. You're practicing for 3-hours. You're grinding in the weight room. It's just the fact that you're on the bus, the plane, in the hotel room together on road trips and that brotherhood of football is something that I've always enjoyed. I most definitely miss game day, but it's those moments leading up to game day that I just mentioned, are those high quality moments that I really enjoyed. To me, that just supersedes all racial lines and socio-economic lines. Nothing brings you together like sports do, more in particular the game of football, which is why I believe that it's the greatest sport in America. Being around the guys, the game and now strictly coaches in what I do for a living, the type of influences that coaches have, I love being a part of that. Other than a dad or a pastor, no person has a bigger impact on a boy than a coach.

I knew football was something I wanted to do for the rest of my life because it has always been something I've done for my life. Once my playing days were over after college, I kicked around the idea of working on the finance, investment or insurance side. Nothing really got my heartbeat going or my adrenaline rushing when I got out of bed every morning. I felt as though that I needed to work in football because I just loved the competition that's involved in the game. Even in what I do now, there's competition because I'm not the only financial planner in the world. How do you bring something different to the table? Well, being a coach's kid, my dad had a lot of integrity, which helped set me up for success. My name is reputable in the industry and I have a commitment to excellence. And being a former walk-on, I understand work ethic; I will not be out-worked. So, putting all of those elements together, I had to figure out how can I both serve and love what I do, and it was a no-brainer to combine that with football by helping coaches.

If I were to write my own football epitaph, it'll have to mention that I finished what I started, never backed down and he played fearlessly from his heart. That is what I think the game of football is all about. I can't stand people that complain about how tough things are; it's almost un-American to me. So from a leadership standpoint, someone has to be the one to step up, so why not me?

John Bland

Head Coach · Mississippi College

www.gochoctaws.com · @ChoctawSports

My dad was my coach and before I started playing football, he played for Mississippi State and played in the NFL for a year or two. Football has been a part of our lives for a long time. As children are being raised, they learn lessons through good parenting; how to make good decisions. It just so happened that my dad was a coach. Not only did he get a chance to teach me lessons, as well as my family, I got a chance to watch him as he coached his team too. I saw him discipline his team and watch his team grow in terms of physical, and mental toughness. I got a chance to watch it as a youngster, but experience it as a player.

I knew that I could always see myself doing that, but I didn't know about it for sure when I got to college. When I got to Arkansas, I started off as a communications major. I wasn't really sure what I was going to do in that, but it sounded good. I knew I had a love for football but I didn't know for sure if that was what I wanted to do. After playing in high school with my dad as my coach, then going to college at Arkansas with Hatfield as my coach, I thought 'You know what? These are really good men. Really good Christian leaders.' I remember the impact they had on so many people and I started to see the big picture. So I changed my major to education in case I was to coach high school ball or college. About that time I realized it was because of the leadership I had from those two that I went into coaching.

The camaraderie of the team is what I love the most. Football is the ultimate team sport in my eyes. One mistake on the field, or off, affects the team so much; there's a lot of accountability. Former players that choose not to coach, but go into business, his days as a football player and the hard work he put in during the offseason, throughout the season, the accountability of making good decisions on, and off the field will carry over to his on-job performance and how he raises his family.

I've got several friends that I played with. I knew them as football players and as friends, and then 20-years later I see them again with their wives and kids. They come up to and say, 'Good to meet you. My husband talks about you and your dad every night at the supper table.' So it makes a difference. It makes an impact not only on the players' lives, but it benefits the players' families. The impact is a lot bigger than we think a lot of times.

You think about all the players that have an impact on you. The ones that got to play on Fridays or Saturdays. But there are thousands of guys that come through your program that may not stay with it for four years. They might have been there for just one semester. The impact that one semester might have is unbelievable. Sometimes I sit back and think about all of the players and the guys that played for my dad that are now having kids are looking to go to college.

Some of them stop by to see me. The stories that they tell and the impact that my dad made on them, that's kind of my goal. I don't think I'll ever reach it to be honest with you. I'm not trying to be my father or Ken Hatfield, but I learned an awful lot from them. I'd like to make an impact on players' lives. My goal is for my players to be glad they got a chance to play for me. Whether we won or lost, I want them to be glad they played the game of football and I want them to feel as though they couldn't have picked a better coach than John Bland.

BRENNAN MARION

OFFENSIVE ASSISTANT - ARIZONA STATE UNIVERSITY
WWW.THESUNDEVILS.COM - @COACHMILKMAN412

At a very young age growing up in Pittsburgh, Pennsylvania where I'm from, football is everything with the Steelers tradition. It's a tough blue-collar town so everybody's into football, that's the main thing. I believe the Steelers have been sold out for the last twenty or thirty years. Playing in the backyard with my uncle and older brother, they put the football in my hands ever since I could remember and we would just play ball and different things. I'd get back there in the backyard and work on my skills. Growing up in the projects, that was the big sport. Everybody played football and you would think it was rough trying to be in a place like that but as a kid, it was a great forum that builds competitiveness. You get a whole bunch of kids playing in the area and you get to play with kids older than you, which make you a little bit better trying to keep up with kids that are older than you or the same age. I started playing at six years old and I played on the seven year old team.

A funny story about me starting to play football is that my mom couldn't afford the twenty-five dollars it cost for me to play, but my brother and uncle kept begging her to let me play. They told her how good I was and the coach told her how good I was because he had seen me do some summer workouts with them. She finally budged and gave me the money to play and my first day I scored five touchdowns with a pair of soccer cleats on, some shin guards, and the big lineman BIKE helmet. I knew then I would be a good football player. Until 6th grade, when I stopped playing little league as a kid, I won the championship ever year and was always MVP of the team. I think it came from growing up in those tough neighborhoods, playing with older kids and playing with my older brother and uncle who's seven years older than me. My uncle was actually a division one player, he played at Purdue with Drew Brees when he was there, so I had some talent that I was playing around and got me a lot better.

That was definitely the escape from home life and whatever was going on. My dad was away from me. He and my mom split when I was two or three years old, so football definitely brought a to me a sense of family and a stable environment during football season. I remember my best times as a kid being during football season. I didn't play on a team that was, all black or all white, it was mixed. So I got to go over an Italian kid's house, a black kid's house, and everybody was family. That's the one thing football has always taught me that you get family and get to learn different people's culture from football and you don't have to be stuck. I wasn't stuck in the environment I was in during football season because I had the chance to be with other families and go eat ice cream after games with the coach.

I remember the coach use to take us to his cabin and we would all go up and play, and do things that would get you out of the situation you were in at home. Football was always my escape and I found refuge in football. Every since I was six years old I had notebooks where I wrote down every player who was drafted and wrote down football plays. When I was real young we lived close to where the Steelers practiced and I would go and interview players about how they liked football. I remember sitting there with Levon Kirkland for a whole day and talking football with him and Yancy Thigpen and the old school Steelers, Bam Morris guys like that and just talking football with them. Football gave me a chance to be someone bigger than who I was supposed to be growing up.

The thing that's always resonated with me about football is that my mom always spoke encouragingly to me, but football was my thing and anyone who knows me knows I always had a football with me. We could be at a basketball court and I would be like okay lets play football. It doesn't matter where I was; I was always playing football and always had a football with me. I knew what my talent level was in football so when I started moving to rougher neighborhoods where people weren't playing football, I started doing what they were doing. I had to make sure that I could survive in those neighborhoods. So in 7th, 8th and 9th grade I played half a season; 10th grade I didn't play because my cousin got shot at school and I transferred schools; 11th grade, I played half a year because of grades, so I didn't play a full season of football until my senior year. My senior year I received all conference and all the accolades that come along with playing, but I didn't have the grades from transferring. I probably went to four different middle schools and five different high schools. So that's almost ten schools from 6th to 12th grade. I just didn't have the grades to go straight into a Division 1 school, so I headed out to go to junior college. I knew right then I had the skills to play at a Division 1 school, I just didn't know the right steps it took to get there. I started meeting people when I was out in California. I went to junior college at Foothill where I met a guy who played for the Raiders, James, and got a chance to train with him and his Receivers coach who was at Fresno State at the time. I could keep up with James and I saw his work ethic and how they worked every day, so I just started making that my work ethic, started working out seven days a week and taking care of myself in the classroom. I had the chance to meet some great mentors who helped me in the classroom and helped me stay eligible. I even spent a little time homeless out there in California and was still able to become an All-American because I knew in the back of my mind that I had the talent, I just needed to do the little things to get me there.

I think having that championship mindset ever since I was a little kid was key. When you win championships, no matter at what level, you feel like you can do anything. I knew in football I was always a champion. I just needed to do the little things and get those things situated to take care of my football dreams.

I tried to work a desk job because when you are use to making six figures, and you go to be a high school or junior college coach, the pay is a 'little' different. A junior college coach was the first opportunity that I got and I think it was a $3,000 stipend or something like that. So I started my own training company and I was doing very well. I was probably making five, six, seven grand a month training kids but I felt like I couldn't control any of the results they had on the field, or as people because I only get them for a little bit of time. I knew that as a football coach, I'd have them for like four to five hours a day. So I got into coaching just to give back all of the things that were given to me as far as, making me a great man and giving me great opportunities and great experiences. I wanted to give that back to kids and teach them that anything is possible. You know with the new generation, a lot of guys getting into high school football coaching who got hurt or their career didn't go the way they wanted it to, and even though mine didn't end on my terms, it ended in surgery and pain, but to me it was bigger than that. I feel like I owe football my life. I have a tattoo that says 'Thank God for the Ball that saved my Life.' I felt like I owed my entire life to football, and the only way to give back was to coach; and tell kids anything is possible and that if you work hard and do the things you need to do, you can be good at this.

One thing that making it to the professional level taught me is that it doesn't matter what college you go to. A lot of kids get wrapped up in what school they go to. There were people on the Dolphins that went to schools that you never heard of and people who didn't even go to college. When I went to the Montreal Alouettes, it was the same thing. They were playing professional just because they believed in themselves and believed in their dreams. That was my biggest thing I wanted to give back to kids what football gave to me throughout my life and kept me going, kept me motivated, got me educated, got me a degree from a private university.

I'm able to sustain in my life, I'm able to go wherever I want, and do whatever I want because I understand and have experience. Football has helped me meet childhood idols. I had an hour conversation with Bill Parcels; Joe Theisman told me I was one of his favorite players before; I sat down and had dinner at Morton's with Franco Harris. These are great things that football has done for me and I try to give that knowledge back to kids. I've tried to get other players, when they were finished playing, to come coach and they are not into it. I just don't understand why you can't be into something that's given so much to you. Because, for me, football is all I've got.

JIM LIGHT

SPECIAL ASSISTANT COACH - DAKOTA HIGH SCHOOL (MI)
WWW.JAMESLIGHTFOOTBALL.COM - @JAMESALIGHT

The first exposure for a lot of people is the NFL Films stuff. All of that stuff makes the game seem almost mythical to you at that point. You grow a love and passion for the game from there to when you first put on the pads and play a little league game.

It's something that never leaves you whether it's coaching, scouting, breaking down film, you grow a passion for the game and it creates something inside of you that you can't replace. Nothing can replace what you get from football.

The competition for starters, there's teamwork, preparation. There's so much that goes into what it takes to win a football game. There is no other sport like it where you have to have a group of 11 guys on the field working together. There's so much that goes into winning a game. A lot of other sports, you play more than you practice. There's so much more preparation that goes into football. It's so satisfying at the end of the game to put it all together and win. There's satisfaction of leaving it all on the line and the preparation and still being able to win.

I tried to give back to football everything that it gave me. I tried to never cheat the game and give everything back and put into it what I feel it gave me. Anyone that will listen, I tell them what football did for me off the field. I am as strong of an advocate for football as anybody could be for the sport. There are a lot of things that you learn on the field that translate to life that you just don't get doing things other than football.

ALBERTA FITCHEARD-BRYDSON
WIDE RECEIVER - DALLAS ELITE (WFA)
WWW.DALLASELITEFOOTBALL.COM - @BERTAB24

I am the only girl in my family in my age group. All of my cousins are boys. That's who I hung with and played with every summer. All of us were getting together playing football and basketball out front in the yard.

I keep learning. If I am still learning and I am still coachable, I feel like my game can keep getting better, why would I walk away? I am learning something new and different every year. There would be this void that I don't even know how I would feel. Every season around January, I start getting real edgy. It's because my body and my brain is transitioning to that football mentality. You have to walk a different way when you step out on that field. With all of the aggression that I start to get as we get closer to the season, I wonder what I would do without football. I want to grow this sport to where we don't have to pay to play and get the sport on a more national level. I meet people every day that don't know that women play football. I love being out there in front of crowds with people cheering for me.

I want to say the adrenaline rush is what I love most about the game. You can be yourself, if you have some pent up aggression, you can release it. You don't have to be too feminine; you can act a fool, talk trash and do things that aren't allowed in society. It's the freedom, that's what it is, the freedom.

I would want my football epitaph to read that I was a competitor, passionate, a leader, teammate and champion. Everyone wants to be a champion; I've had the opportunity to be a champion four times. It's amazing when you lead and you're not trying to lead. People just come to you. That's something that I have in me. You have to have passion in whatever you are doing in order to be successful.

SCOTT BUTERA

COMMISSIONER - ARENA FOOTBALL LEAGUE
WWW.ARENAFOOTBALL.COM - @AFLCOMMISH

I played sports from the time I was a little boy. I played baseball but I was a bigger kid. I always wanted to play pop warner football but I couldn't make it because I was big early. I loved the contact, the excitement and the speed of the game. When I got into high school, I focused all of my attention on football. I played all through high school and college and it was the most memorable times of my life. It was a great release after a frustrating day to be able to go out there and knock it around a little bit. It was good to exert some energy and let some steam out. There's nothing like the whole aspect from practice, to getting together the night before a game, to riding the bus to games, it's almost like a religion. It brings us together as people. The sport of football, you look at society and the problems that we still have regarding diversity, on the football field, everyone is your brother. No matter where they are from, what their background is, who their parents are or what neighborhood they're from, it just doesn't matter. You are all in it together. You are all equal, striving for the same goal. Everybody should experience that. If we played football and transferred it to life, the world would be a better place.

I worked on Wall Street for 25 years and I worked in the gaming industry for a very long time. Every business meeting I had, I always started out talking about football. I always wanted to get back into the sport. I always paid attention to what was going on. Joining the Arena Football League was an opportunity to get involved in the sport. The speed and the excitement, the hard-hitting in the game is what I love. It's a very fast, hard-hitting game.

I'd like my impact on the game to be that I made a difference for a collection of athletes that may not have gotten the opportunity that they should have gotten. We have scholarship programs for athletes that played in our league to help them get back to college and get their degrees. I want to create a great opportunity for the people that are involved with us and help them develop.

Alex Kirby

Football Coach & Author

www.lifeafterfootballblog.com - @AlexJKirby

Well, I guess the first place to start is that my family was not a 'sports family.' No one that I could think of was ever into sports or really played sports. So it was kind of a weird thing when I got involved and picked up on this. Honestly, the first place that I got any serious contact with the game of football was the Madden football video games. We didn't grow up with much and I still had a Super Nintendo when a lot of guys had a Sony Playstation. So I just picked up the Madden '96, started playing and was like 'man, I really like this.' I'm the type of person that feels that you have to actually 'do' something in order to get a true feel for it, but at that time, that was the closest I could get to it without actually playing. That's when I fell in love with football. I started watching it on TV not long after that, I got more into it and been in love ever since.

I would say that I knew right away that this would be something that I wanted to do or at least be a large part of my life. The first thing that appealed to me was the strategy of it because I always like those types of games. But also the toughness factor is what appealed to me as well. I grew up in a very religious family. I actually grew up as a Jehovah's Witness. Because of that, I was not allowed to play football or hardly any extra-curricular activities. That's why I never played football. I fought with my parents about that for a long time, starting in about 7th grade. And then when I got to high school, I convinced them to let me be a part of the school's radio team that broadcasted the games. I was the color-commentator, which gave me access to the coaching staff and they actually gave me film to watch on the upcoming opponent that week. That's how I got my first exposure and experience in breaking down film.

In my senior year, I then convinced my parents to let me be an actual video guy for the team. So I wasn't playing, but I was around the staff. I knew the offense, the defense and special teams. That was my first time being around an actual team and I loved it! It was everything that I thought it would be. After graduation, I stuck around and actually worked my way up to a varsity assistant coach.

I'd be lying if I said that I wasn't a little upset about not playing but I do think there are definite advantages in doing it the way I did. Obviously there's no injuries or medical issues that I have to deal with. The other thing is that I got into the coaching side of it right away at 19 years old basically. Some of the best guys I've ever met have been football coaches or just coaches in general. So I was lucky in that respect to be around some really good guys that were looking out for me. But once I got to about 22-23 years old, you get these guys coming out of college who are about the same age as me but I have 4 years more coaching experience than they do. So to me, I would have loved to have played, but at the same time I did get a great head start in the coaching arena than a lot of other people.

BOB MCMILLEN
HEAD COACH - LOS ANGELES KISS
WWW.LAKISSFOOTBALL.COM - @LAKISS_AFL

I think as a kid, you just wanted to hang out with your friends and a lot of my friends at the time played sports. A few of them said, 'hey lets go out for the football team.' I went to a catholic grade school and we just so happened to have a team. So in the 5th grade we all went out for the team. We didn't know anything about the game but we sure did have a great time playing it.

I was a running back in grade school and by the time I made it to high school, I was a defensive back. As I went on to college I played tight end, and in the Arena Football League I played fullback. So I changed positions so many times. But I think the success that I had at an early age, especially as a running back, it motivated me to keep playing. I made an all-star team then and by the time I got to high school, I started getting some looks from college recruited and also kept me really engaged in the game. I said this is what I want to do and I kept on pursuing it.

The fans and how passionate they are about the game is something that I really love about the game of football. Just seeing how excited they get during a game is exciting. I grew up a Chicago Bears fan and my favorite player was Walter Payton. Just watching him play and how he did things on and off the field was something that I thought if I ever made a name for myself, that's how I'd want to be. I wanted to emulate what he did and how he did it. He played when he was injured and did what he could off the field for his charities. All of that just made me want to do more and play more football.

If I had to write what I'd want my football legacy to say, it'll say that I may not have been the best, but I gave it my all. Don't ever let anyone tell you that you can't do something because I'm one of those people that'll always prove you wrong. I wasn't the greatest, best, or fastest athlete but I was going to give you everything that I had on a football field, whether it was in practice or in games. That's how I approached and played every game from grade school, to the professional ranks.

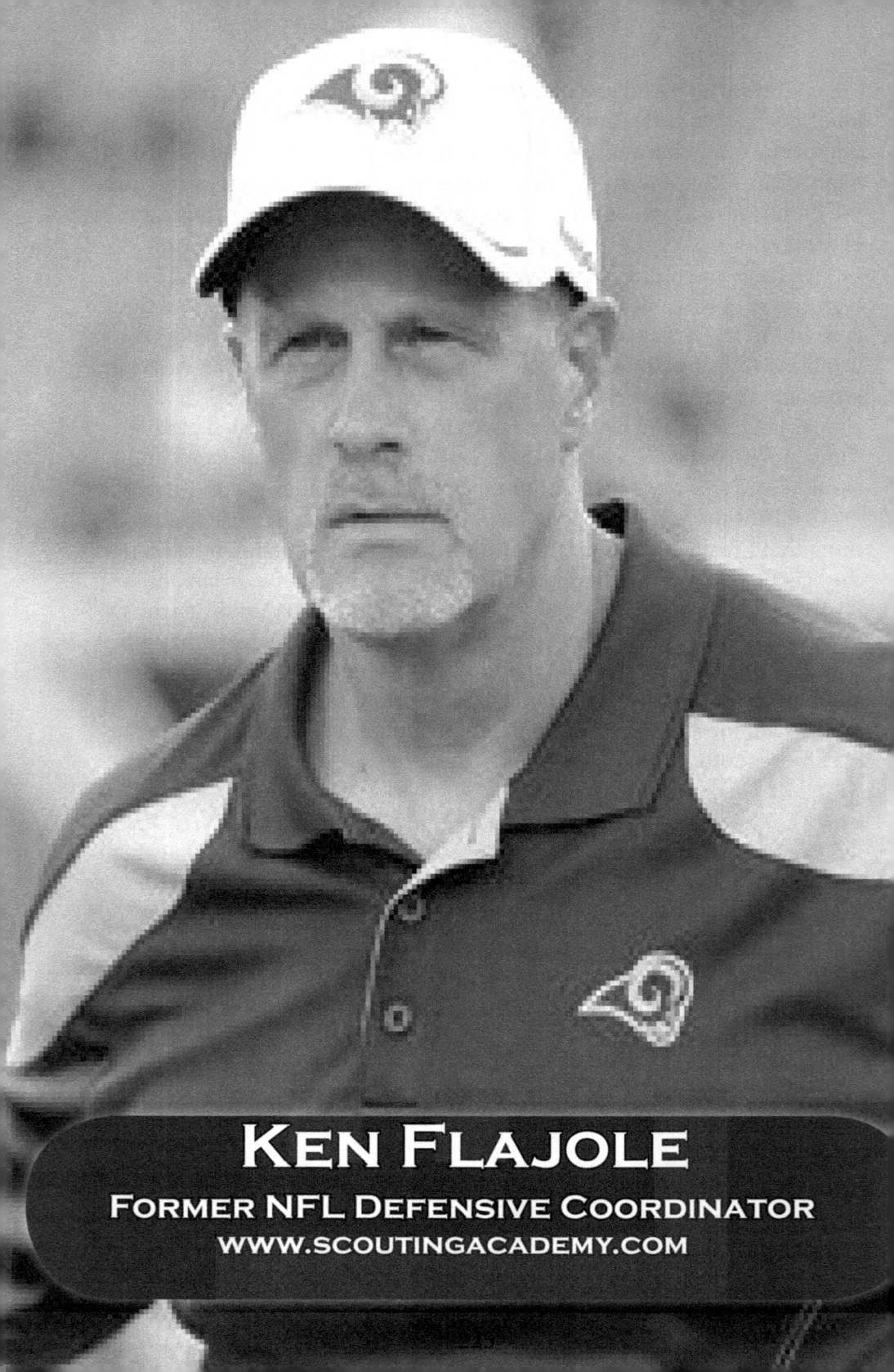

Ken Flajole
Former NFL Defensive Coordinator
WWW.SCOUTINGACADEMY.COM

I always enjoyed the special bond in the game of football between the players. I played at a small college, but we had a great group of people that were on our team. That special bond that exists between teammates, particularly in the sport of football, was unique. That was sort of the beginning of what caught my attention initially. The more I did it, the more I enjoyed the game and wanted to be involved with it past playing; and my career took that path.

I kind of figured it out before I left college that I wanted football to be my career. I enjoyed playing the game. And as for coaching the game, I like the strategy and intricacies of it. All of those things sort of drew me into it more. I think the thing that probably gave me longevity was that I was blessed to be around a bunch of really good people that were players that I enjoyed coaching. These are guys that I've remained close to and friends with over the course of 37 years of coaching, 21 in college football and 16 in the NFL.

Coaching is an ever-changing job; it's never the same thing everyday. So there's no boredom factor. I really enjoyed being around the players. When you get to be an old guy like me, being around the players really keeps you young. You are constantly around young people that are in the prime of their lives physically. To be around them and feed off of them with their energy and enthusiasm, it keeps an older guy a young guy. Even in pro football, I think a lot of people think that it's a business not like it is in high school and in college, but that's not necessarily true. You get close to a lot of those guys; you get to know them and their families. And that becomes an important part of what you do and why you do it.

At the professional level, even at the college level, football is a chess match. There's always things that are happening and many different ebbs and flows to a game. I used to work with a guy that said, 'you're always working for those 6-8 definitive plays in a game.' Whether you're on the offensive, defensive or special teams side, there's always those 6-8 plays that are key points in a game; and the strategy of how you get to those particular plays, and the execution of them, is always a drawing effect to why you do the things you do. his best to work each and every day.

That's what I really enjoyed about the game. The constant cat-and-mouse game of 'if they do this, then I'll do this.' There's always something going on which keeps it exciting. The constant back and forth; then there's an unknown factor thrown in like an injury and all of a sudden, you have to adjust on the fly. So, it's never a mundane task! It's always evolving and changing and that's the fun part of it.

You hope that as a coach, the players know that you cared about them more as an individual than the wins and losses. You also want to be known as a someone who was both proficient and able in your job, who brought his best to work each and every day.

KATIE ROSE

TEAM USA WOMEN'S TACKLE FOOTBALL PLAYER

I grew up watching football. My entire family were Redskins' fans growing up. I always wanted to play. I didn't know that as a girl that I wouldn't be able to play. I just figured they wouldn't know I was a girl once I put on my helmet, so as far as I knew, I was always going to play football. I love the contact. I love tackling and I love being tackled, I love the hits, I enjoy being allowed to be that physical.

I don't think women have that issue, but the level that we play hasn't been reduced to physical violence such as head hits and spearing. It's still more pure at the women's level. I think that the physical hits haven't turned into violence. It's more of a clash than assassination.

I would hope for my impact to be that I was influential in the game of football and that I was able to do whatever my team needed me to do; and I had a hand in bringing the sport of women's football to people so that women had an opportunity to play.

J.C. MORGAN

Offensive Coordinator - Shippensburg University
www.shipraiders.com - @CoachJCMorgan

I grew up in a small town in Middletown, Delaware and football was everything back then. On Friday night, the town would shut down as everybody went out to watch the local high school game. I just remember being very young watching those guys play and how everybody in town put those guys on a pedestal and that was neat. So my cousins and I as youngsters dreamt of playing in that high school stadium and being the talk of the town. We were very successful and that played a big part in it but that's what initially drew me into the game of football. We had a great youth organization and just the attention that came with it, got us excited about playing.

I felt like football was always in my blood. Even as a high school student-athlete, I really got involved in coaching. I was a youth league coach while I was in high school. The strategy, the X's and O's, I mean you could ask my mom about my school notebook and she'll tell you that it had nothing but X's and O's all over it. I just always thought in the back of my mind that it would be great to be a coach. The way I looked up to coaches when I was a young man, I just thought that it would be cool to have that type of impact on young people's lives when I got to that stage. That's ultimately how I was able to get involved with it and even through my college years as my body started breaking down as a junior, going into my senior year I was coaching at a high school while still in college finishing up my undergrad degree. Even coaching at the high school level for that one year, I just couldn't get it out of my system. So by the time I was graduating college, I knew exactly what I wanted to do. I had a business degree but the shirt and tie aspect didn't sit well with me. I wanted to be on a whiteboard, in the film room and on a football field. So, I can't imagine doing anything different than what I'm doing right now.

Hands down it's the competition that I love the most about the game of football. Whether it's a drill, 1-on-1s or 7-on-7s, it's just the idea of competing, talking a little noise while you compete, it's just a lot of fun. When there's a specific play or specific drive that determines a winner or a loser, that's exciting. Obviously the important parts of practice as a coach are the individual periods because, that's when you get the chance to teach. That's when you get the guys ready for the team periods. But when it's time to compete, I think it just kicks up a notch and the arena of competition just gets me going.

I would want my legacy to live through the young men that I've coached. And by having me be a part of their life, they were better because of it. Look, there's going to be wins and losses, hopefully you win more than you lose, but at the end of the day, if a young man can say that by dealing with me during their college experience that became a better husband, father, and member of the community, that would mean the world to me. I think sometimes, can get lost in the shuffle a little bit when you're going through the day-to-day grind. But I know the impact that coaches had on me as I developed into a young man, so if I can have the same impact on them, that would mean the world to me.

CHRIS JAMES

NFL DRAFT ANALYST - FOOTBALL GAMEPLAN
WWW.FOOTBALLGAMEPLAN.COM - @CJFLORIDA9

I'd always watch it on TV at my grandma's house and used to tell her that she would be watching me one day. So I started playing football in junior high school. It was a tough time in my life so I took a break from it for a year. I was drawn back in during high school and I found my niche at wide receiver. After I was done playing I still kept talking about the game. It didn't matter the setting or the situation, I would find a way to bring up the game. That's when I knew that this was something I wanted to do for long time.

As cliché as it sounds, I love the way football allows everyone to come together in pursuit of a common goal. All races, colors, creeds, etc. can learn to be part of a team in pursuit of success, or at the very least, cheer their team to victory. The game also allows you to forget about the trials and tribulations of your life for 3 or so hours at a time. You become intoxicated by the game and it inspires euphoria when you get the win.

I just hope that after it's all said and done, people will say that I knew football was a simple game played by complex people.

WILL HALL

HEAD COACH - UNIVERSITY OF WEST GEORGIA
WWW.UWGSPORTS.COM - @COACH_HALL7

My dad is one of the most successful high school football coaches in the eastern part of the state of Mississippi; and he's still coaching. He's won 4 state titles, 298 games and will probably reach 300 victories this year. He has always been a program builder, going to a place that hadn't won a lot and turning it around; he'd win and win big. I just always saw how he impacted lives but also how he really invigorated communities by giving them so much pride and providing them with something that they could believe in. I always admired my dad and knew at a young age I wanted to be a football coach. I started going to the field house maybe in kindergarten, and have been going ever since.

I knew at a young age that I probably wasn't going to be the tallest guy. I was fortunate to have a really good career as a quarterback. I was lucky to maximize my playing career to the fullest, but I always knew in the back of my mind that if I wanted to have a career in football, it'd have to be in coaching.

I love that with the game of football, you have such a huge impact on young peoples lives. Even more so in some ways, we could reach and touch more young lives than even a pastor. But besides that, I really love the X's and O's of the game. I'm a math guy and that's kind of the way my brain works. There are so many moving pieces and just the schematics of it are just more in-depth than any other sport. I've always been intrigued with game planning and putting people in the right place to be successful.

I hope when I'm dead and gone that people say, 'Man that dang Will Hall, every time I came in contact with him, my day was better than any time I didn't come in contact with him.' I think we impact people that we come in contact with on a daily basis. So I just hope that when people run into me that their day is better because of it.

BRYAN KEYS

DEFENSIVE LINEMAN - GREEN BAY BLIZZARD (IFL)
WWW.GREENBAYBLIZZARD.COM - @KINGKEYS77

Basketball was my first sport. In my youth league days I made the decision that I wanted to be active, so at first I chose to do basketball competitively. My 1st head coach at the time, Joe Mallett, made a deal with my dad. "I'll let him play basketball if I can have him for a year a football." In my eyes it was an easy two for one.

I love the unknown of football. I love that the game is unforgiving and it holds every one accountable for their decisions. Nothing is guaranteed and whatever is guaranteed is a lie.

I was in my Junior year of high school when I realized that football is what I wanted to do for a career. After having people tell you for two years that you're pretty good, it finally dawned on me. I remember waking up one morning from school and telling myself "let's go the distance, let's become the guy that you are supposed to be." From then on my attitude changed, and so did my work habits. I just want to be in the NFL so bad and I'll keep fighting until that day comes. I don't care about 0.1% that makes it. At the end of the day it's all on me and I don't mind betting on myself. I like those odds a lot better than the 0.1% that tries to generalize my mindset.

I want my legacy to be that he took the most untraditional path and still found a way to make it. He beat out politics, he beat out what the experts said, and he defeated any negativity coming from himself and anyone around him.

Gene Clemons

Coach, Author, Analyst at Football Gameplan
www.footballgameplan.com - @geneclemons

As a kid, my brother was my idol. I wanted to do anything he was doing. He was the original reason why I began to play basketball and subsequently, he was the reason why I began to play football. I followed him everywhere. And when he would play 'throw it up tackle' in the vacant lots in Chicago, I would play with him. My adolescence was spent playing sandlot with my brother and his friends, which really sparked my love for the game.

I knew the first time I put on pads that I wanted to be involved with football in some capacity for the rest of my life. I didn't play regulation football until 9th grade and in my eight seasons of prep and college football, I played under four head coaches and six offensive coordinators. It wasn't necessarily the healthiest thing for winning games to have such turnover, but I learned a lot of football in a short amount of time, and it made me a sponge for information. I credit it with my quick transition into coaching. I went in with a knowledge base far beyond those players with a stable coaching situation in their playing career. I fell in love with the chess match that's involved in football. I was obsessed with not only winning, but also learning how to anticipate the opponents' moves. No other sport gives you a chance to be that cerebral on a large scale.

A coach once called me, "a football dude" and I thought it was the best compliment ever. I consider myself to be a football dude and that's what I would want to be remembered for. A guy who knew the game, approached it the right way, and didn't take shortcuts.

TENEL CURTIS

OWNER/CEO - AMBITIOUS 365 & (DIMW) DID IT MY WAY LLC

PARTNER - THE TASTE OF JAZZ SAUCE COMPANY LLC
WWW.AMBITIOUS365.COM - IG: @TKURTIZ

I grew up watching the New Orleans Saints games every Sunday and always acted like I was a member of the Dome Patrol. As a kid, I was to heavy into playing park ball with my age group so every day after school, I would go home and get the guys on my block to play one hand touch in the streets until I made it to high school and was able to participate in full contact football.

What do I love about the game of football? That's an easy answer for me. It's the ability to inflict pain onto others. It's the ability to take another mans will to move or play the next down, and to make the person in front me say enough.

"*The teamwork of young kids getting after it on the field is what initially drew me into the game of football. When you see kids get to achieve their dreams, like moving on to play Division I or onto the NFL, and most importantly moving on to achieve their educational goals, makes coaching all the worthwhile.*"

- *Tom Minnick*
Head Coach, Arizona Western C.C.

If They Don't Have Football In Heaven
•••• I'M NOT GOING ••••

About Football Gameplan

FOOTBALL GAMEPLAN LLC: Established in 2007, Football Gameplan.com is the one-stop shop for the football fanatic providing in-depth analysis on the NFL, NFL Draft, College Football (FBS,FCS,D2,D3,NAIA,-JUCO), Canadian Football League, Canadian College Football, CFL Draft, Arena Football, Indoor Football, Women's Tackle Football, International Football, High School Football, Recruiting, Minor League Football, Coaching & Scouting Tips.

FOOTBALL GAMEPLAN RADIO NETWORK: Established in 2011, the Football Gameplan Radio Network consists of 12 different LIVE podcasts covering the different leagues. All of the podcasts are downloadable on iTunes. To see a list of the shows, visit www.footballgameplan.com/radio-network

FOOTBALL GAMEPLAN UNIVERSITY: Established in 2014, Football Gameplan University is a traveling coaches clinic. Whether it's on a high school or college campus, or pro facility, FBGPU brings you great video interviews and whiteboard coaching segments from across the globe.

GAMEPLAN: Established in 2011, Gameplan is our own whiteboard instructional video segments designed to explain the finer points of the game to the novice, while also offering tools and tips of the trade to the advanced in order to help you win on game day.

FOOTBALL GAMEPLAN SCOUTING: Established in 2015, FBGP Scouting brings you detailed scouting information. From high school prospect evaluations to all-22 film session evaluations of college prospects across the country. The FBGP staff gives you their grades and scouting reports on players in the pro game (NFL, CFL, AFL, Indoor) as well. This is a subscription service.
Find out more information at www.footballgameplan.com/FBGPScouting

FOOTBALL GAMEPLAN NETWORK: Established in 2009, the FBGP Network is Football Gameplan's YouTube channel which has over 40 original programs and has over 4.5 million organic views and 9,500 subscribers.

FOOTBALL GAMEPLAN PUBLISHING: Established in 2014, FBGP Publishing provides great reading content from motivational books to coaching instruction in addition to original feature items.
Visit www.footballgameplan.com/Books to check out our library.

FBGP Social Media

TWITTER:
@FBallGameplan
@FBGPScouting
@FBGPUniversity
@FBGPRadioNetwork
@GameplanXO

FACEBOOK:

Football Gameplan Fan Page: facebook.com/football-gameplan

YOUTUBE:

Football Gameplan Network: YouTube.com/FootballGameplan

INSTAGRAM:

@FootballGameplan

GOOGLE PLUS

FBGPNetwork

PINTEREST:

FBallgameplan

Be sure to check out our latest book: *Stiff Arming Football Myths*
www.footballgameplan.com/BOOKS
Available in Paperback & PDF

www.ingramcontent.com/pod-product-compliance
Lightning Source LLC
Chambersburg PA
CBHW031949090426
42739CB00006B/124